Life Death

Or

Somewhere

In-between.

True Paramedic Stories.

By Patrick Ramsey

I dedicate this book to all those that serve and have served the public as a Paramedic, EMT, Firefighter, or Law Enforcement Officer.

I want to thank my wife Tracey for encouraging me to write and publish this book.

Tracey along with Shawn, our son, also helped me edit this book. I couldn't have done it without them.
Thank you.

Table of Contents:

Preface….How it all Started

"What is the most gruesome thing you have ever seen?"

"Why do you do it?"

"Aren't you afraid of catching something?"

"How do you stay up all night?"

"Have you ever delivered a baby?"

"How many dead people have you seen at once?"

"Does it upset you to see a baby die?"

These are some of the more common questions asked when people discover you have been or are a paramedic. I am sure people want to ask more direct questions but are probably too polite to ask. I will attempt to answer these questions and many more in this book.

It all started in 1975 when, as a member of a small rural Texas volunteer fire department, I raised my hand and voted to start an ambulance division within the fire department.

I had no idea how that vote would change my life as well as many other people's lives over the next 25 years.

I was actively involved in all of the incidents in this book. Of course many other people were also involved. My partners along with fire departments, rescue squads, and law enforcement made up a team of people with the same general goal, to help people in distress. On many occasions, private citizens who just wanted to help stopped and offered their assistance and made the difference in someone's life.

I have seen the best of human behavior and unfortunately the worst. As I mentioned people offering to help an accident victim even though they were scared and unsure as to what they should or could do. In the same night finding two people dead and another wounded from gun shoot wounds after a dispute about money.

I came to the conclusion early in my emergency medical career that the two best traits a paramedic can possess are a sense of humor and common sense. Yes, a sense of humor. Humor gets you through the bad times and helps you cope. Finding the humor in a call may seem inappropriate but some calls are funny, read on and see what I mean. Contrary to popular belief not every call is a life or death struggle; in fact most of the people transported by ambulances would do just fine if they went to the hospital in a car. Today's society has taught people to call 911 if they need help. Needing help has a broad definition to people. To some people it means waiting until a family member passes out from blood loss before calling EMS. To others it means calling at 3:00 A.M. be transported to the emergency room for a stomachache they've had for two days. You arrive at their house to find them standing in the front yard waiting with their overnight bag in hand. Sometimes you laugh just to keep from crying.

Having common sense, being able to think on your feet, separates the good paramedics from the mediocre. A paramedic can be book smart, knowing exactly what drug or treatment to administer in any given situation. If someone's heart stops they can run the algorithm forward and backward to revive him. What you don't learn in school is the person you are trying to revive might weigh 300 pounds and be wedged between the toilet and the wall in the back bathroom of a trailer home that has 20 years of junk piled up in the hall. Then after you do finally to get enough help on the scene to drag this patient to the door you have to negotiate rickety wooden stairs that are four feet high because the owner got a bargain on the land since it's on a hill. Believe me you haven't lived until you've backed down those stairs carrying the stretcher and patient trying to maintain your balance while the stairs sway about one foot from side to side.

In small rooms I have taken doors off hinges so we would have enough space to get the patient out. I have handed patients out windows because it was almost impossible to get them out of the room any other way. I commandeered a forklift at a mobile home factory to lower the patient from the roof he was decking. By the way, the man had shot himself in the knee with the pneumatic nail gun. He missed the roof and hit his knee. I questioned him as to how you miss something as big as a roof and hit your knee instead. He didn't have an answer. I had an answer, it is what I and other paramedics call a lapse of intelligence or as most people call it, doing something dumb. We all do dumb things; unfortunately it sometimes gets us a ride to the hospital in the ambulance. This is a book about some of the dumb, sad, unfortunate, funny, gut retching, and interesting calls I have been involved in.

These stories cover a time span of over twenty years. Since they are timeless I have purposely left out references to when they occurred. This also makes it harder to find out the real names of the patients. Yes, I changed them, something about patient confidentiality. The locations are real and so is time of day or night and the season that they happened. To hopefully put the reader "there" I wrote the stories in first person present tense.

The idea of writing this book came about many years ago. I would tell "war stories" about a call or calls I had been involved in, usually after being asked one of the aforementioned questions. Many people through the years would say. "You should write a book." I decided I would someday do just that. I started making notes and did so for years about the interesting calls I made. This book was written using those notes.

I have tried to be as accurate as I can about what happened and most of all what was said at the time. Of course this means it is my version as I remember it. In some cases I discussed the call with my old partners to see if my memory of the event jived with theirs and adjusted the story accordingly. Others involved might have different views of what happened but like I said I have tried to be as accurate as I can.

Chapter One….Birthing Babies

In my opinion of all the experiences you can have as a paramedic delivering a healthy baby is the most fun. I have to give credit to the mothers, they did all the work and my partner and I got the glory.

The First One

A young unwed mother goes into labor; her brother helps her to the car and heads for the hospital. Their mother works at a dry cleaners located in a strip center. Since the cleaner is on the way to the hospital they decide to stop and pick up Mom and then proceed to the hospital.

Big brother parks the car and runs in to get Mom. In the few moments it takes for them to get out to the car sister's water has broken and pushing time has arrived. Mom realizes getting to the hospital before the baby is born is not going to happen. She decides to call for an ambulance.

I arrive on the scene to find future Mom lying across the back seat of the car. A quick check of the patient reveals she is crowning. This means the top of the baby's head is already showing. I realize we will barely have time to get her into the ambulance before the baby is delivered much less get her to the hospital. I tell my partner to get the stretcher and turn my attention to the patient who is rightfully scared to death. "What is your name?"

"Jean."

"Ok Jean how far along are you?" I ask.

"Do what?" She replies.

"How many months along are you? When is the baby due?" I ask trying to simplify my question.

"I been carryin' this child fo' nine months now."

"Jean, listen to me. You are only a few minutes from having this baby. We won't have time to get to the hospital. We are going to put you in the ambulance and deliver the baby there."

Everyone is excited. I thought, "hot dog! I am going to get to deliver my first baby." The patients Mom was excited, it's her first grandchild. Her brother is excited; he's about to become an Uncle. More scared than excited about the prospect of having a baby is the future Mom. I do what I can to reassure her she is in good hands but a 16 year old having her first baby while lying in the back of an old un-air-conditioned Chevy kind of loses her perspective of things. Between contractions we quickly move the patient to the stretcher and into the ambulance.

My partner thinking ahead opens the cabinet where the O.B. kit is stored grabs it and starts wrestling with the package. O.B. being short for obstetrical kit is a sealed plastic bag containing clamps, towels, scalpel, bulb suction, and sterile gloves. Everything needed to deliver a baby. She finally tears it open and the contents fly to the four corners of the back of the ambulance, "Looks like I'm not the only one that's excited" I thought.

In the few seconds that it takes to find the gloves and put them on, the patient is having another contraction. I can now see the baby's head starting to emerge. I know in few more minutes the babies' head will be out. I try to calm down and concentrate on what all needs to be done. Even though this appears to be a normal birth I know that several things can go wrong. Some of the possible complications that cross my mind are: The umbilical cord could be wrapped around its neck, the baby might not start breathing, the placenta could tear loose from the uterine wall and the patient could bleed to death. These are some of the possible complications that cross my mind as I prepare to deliver the baby.

Another contraction and the baby's head delivers. "Good," I think, "the umbilical cord isn't around its neck and the baby is already trying to breathe". As the next contraction starts I help the shoulders get clear. I expect another contraction before the baby is fully delivered but to my surprise after the shoulders clear the baby just sort of slides on out. Even though I had watched babies delivered in my clinical training I didn't remember them being born so quickly. It finally dawned on me several years later. The reason we get to deliver them in the ambulance is because it is usually an easy birth, the mothers that are in labor for 12 hours make it to the hospital.

I lay the baby across my arm face down and quickly suction out her nose and mouth with a bulb syringe. I want to get all the fluid out of the baby's airway before I get her to take a deep breath. After getting the airway clear I thump the brand new baby girl on the bottom of her feet so she will take a deep breath. It only takes a few to get her to start crying loud and clear. As far as I know it is only in the movies that they hold a slippery new born up in the air by its ankles and smack its bottom. Finally I clamp the cord and cut it.

The new mom is now starting to realize she has had a baby and starts asking the usual questions. "Is it a boy or a girl? Is it ok? Can I hold her?"

Shirley, my partner, wraps the baby in a towel and lets the new mother hold her.

Now that most of the work is done. The placenta still has to be delivered but that usually doesn't happen for 15 minutes or so. I decide to go outside and tell the new grandma and uncle that everything is OK and that we will be transporting soon. I open the back door of the ambulance and to my surprise find a small crowd has gathered to await the good news. "It's a girl; mother and baby are doing fine!" I announce. Upon hearing the news the crowd actually cheers and claps. Something I rarely hear on a call.

Water Baby

Sometimes we don't even make it to the ambulance and end up delivering the baby where we find the mother. The first time this happened I arrived at the address in an upper middle class neighborhood.

It's about three in the afternoon and a nice warm South Texas Spring day. The local fire department is already on the scene as first responders. I enter the house and one of the firefighters tells me the patient is in the bedroom. I head down the hall and into the master bedroom to find the patient laying on a King size waterbed. She appears to be in her late 20s and is relatively calm considering she is in labor and there are 4 people in the room.

The young firefighter attending to her turns to me his eyes wide open with excitement at the prospect of delivering a baby, "She's full term and the labor pains are only one minute apart." He tells me nervously.

I quickly question the mother as I check to see how close she is to actually having the baby. Mom informs me this is her second child and that her first one was delivered after only two hours of labor. "That's pretty quick." I think. She then tells me she's been in labor for about an hour and was waiting for her husband to get home to take her to the hospital. While waiting her water had broken and contractions suddenly went from 5 minutes apart to less than 2. Rightfully guessing that she was not going to make it to the hospital, she called for an ambulance.

In the time it takes to ask and answer these questions, less than a minute, she has another contraction. The top of the baby's head is already crowning. I quickly came to the same conclusion that she had, we are about to deliver this baby at home.

As I mentioned the patient is laying in the middle of a king size waterbed. A problem quickly develops as we try to position ourselves and the patient to deliver the soon to be born child. Anytime anyone, moves or touches the bed, it moves, as waterbeds are prone to do. We all quickly realize that on top of getting seasick it will be extremely difficult to deliver the baby on the waterbed.

I explain to her. "When this contraction stops we are going to pick you up with the sheet and put you on the floor. " My partner, two firefighters, and myself each grab a corner of the sheet and wait for the contraction to stop. When it does we gently lift and then lower her to the floor.

The nervous firefighter, who is also an EMT, had the foresight to bring the OB kit in with him and was the only one wearing gloves. I can see how excited he is at the prospect of delivering a baby so I decide to let him have the honor. "Do you want to deliver the baby?" I ask him. "I will be right here to help if you need it."

"Yeees." He says, becoming even more nervous than before. He no sooner positions himself and another contraction starts. Putting his fingers on the top of the baby's head, he turns and supports it as it is delivered. One more contraction and a new person comes into the world, all in less than 3 minutes of arriving at the house.

After all the customary questions of what sex it is and is he healthy, the mother asks the firefighter if she has any tears or rips. He seems totally flabbergasted by this question and I notice he makes no attempt to answer her. Instead he turns to me and whispers. "I've never seen a woman's privates before I wouldn't know if it was torn or not."

The frankness of his statement takes me totally by surprise and it's all I can do to not to start laughing right then and there. I glance at my partner to see if she heard what he said. She heard it alright and has to look away and busy herself with the baby to keep from laughing. I quickly look and inform the mother that there is a slight tear that should only take a stitch or two to fix.

I realize his nervousness is more than just delivering a baby for the first time. As he put it "seeing a woman's privates" for the first time from that prospective must have be an unforgettable experience for him.

Doing the Dance

Most paramedics like to brag about how many babies they have delivered and I am no different. Although I only delivered six in my career, all of them except one were happy events.

It's just after morning shift change and my partner and I are heading out to eat breakfast. We've just left the station when the cell phone rings.

We had only recently acquired cell phones for our ambulances, one of the neatest gadgets ever invented for EMS. With two-way radios, which are still use for most communications, you have to be extremely careful what you say. In the rural area where I worked at that time many people wanted to know what was going on in the county and monitored the police, fire, and ambulance radio frequencies on scanners. Cell phones are great; with them you can be a little more candid if you need to be. This particular morning the dispatcher saw fit to call us and let us know what was happening in detail rather than the usual "O.B. call at such and such."

As I answer the phone I can hear the dispatcher laughing. I recognize her voice, it's Patty, one of the few dispatchers with a sense of humor.

"Medic 5," I say suspiciously.

Patty, still giggling, asks, "Do you feel like delivering a baby this morning?"

"Sure, why not. Might as well start the day out on a positive note," I answer.

I am skeptical. Most of the time when someone calls and tells the dispatcher they are having a baby and need an ambulance they are nowhere near having it. They just want an easy ride to the hospital. Sometimes they don't have a car or it doesn't have gas or they just figure it will be better to ride in an ambulance and go first class.

Patty sensing that I think it's the usual "cry wolf" O.B. call goes on to inform us that she could hear the mother screaming in the background when her sister called. In her opinion it sounded like someone just about to have a baby.

We get the address; it is only a few blocks away from where we are. We turn the corner and spot the patient's grown sister standing in the yard jumping up and down, waving her arms, and shouting. I call it "doing the dance."

We pull up alongside an old wood frame house in an older section of town. It's what is commonly called a "shotgun house."

Before we even have time to get out of the truck she is running toward the house telling us to hurry.

"Grab the kit," I tell my partner. "I'll go see what's happening."

My regular partner is off and I have a part time employee riding with me. Douglas is a paramedic with years of experience but only works with our company on rare occasions. I just assumed he knew where the O.B. kit was, he didn't.

Following the sister I head for the door and enter the living room. The room is very dark with only one small window and no lights. Since it's a bright day out I have difficulty seeing for a few seconds. All I can make out at first is someone lying on the couch. Judging by her screams she is having a contraction as I walk across the room. My eyes finally start to adjust as I get to the couch and I can see she is about 30 years old. She's wearing a simple straight dress that is up around her waist and no underwear. The couch is soaked with amniotic fluid and the baby's head crowning. Looks like Patty was right, we're going to deliver a baby.

I instinctively place my hand on the baby's head and get ready for the next contraction. "I'm Patrick, I'm a paramedic. Looks like you're going to have this baby right here on the couch," I tell her in my most reassuring voice.

Another contraction starts, "I don't wanna' have this baby in da' house," She tells me between screams.

"We don't have time to get you to the ambulance. Besides I've delivered a bunch of babies at home," I tell her. I realize she probably didn't hear me over her own screaming. The contraction reaches its peak along with her screaming and cussing.

I am now holding the baby's head waiting for the next contraction and wondering where Doug might be. Just then my long lost partner decides to join us. He is carrying the trauma kit but not the O.B. kit. "Uh Doug, I'm about to deliver this baby. Think you could get the O.B. kit?" I ask. Seeing what's about to happen he bolts for the door and heads to the ambulance to get it.

One more contraction accompanied by more screaming and the baby is born. She appears to be normal. Laying her across my arm and holding her in a head down position to drain any fluid in that might be in her nose and mouth; I wait for my partner to come back in with the O.B. kit. I can see the ambulance through the window but no partner. Finally after what seems like a minute or so I see him emerge from the back of the ambulance and run toward the house with the kit.

Doug comes in the door and heads toward the couch. It takes a second for him to realize I have already delivered the baby. He kneels down and attempts to open the O.B. kit. He tears at the plastic bag and finally rips it open. Since the first thing you do after delivering a baby is to suction it I hold out my hand expecting him to hand me the bulb syringe. To my dismay he digs frantically through the bag and produces a scalpel. In an attempt to keep the atmosphere light I ask him in joking manner, "Don't you think we should probably suction her before cutting the cord?" Somewhat embarrassed Doug digs through the bag again finally finding the bulb syringe.

I suction her mouth and nose and thump her feet a few times getting her to take a deep breath and cry for a few moments. "Ok, looking good," I say to the mother, since most want to know if the baby is healthy or not. She doesn't seem to hear me because she is still crying and screaming.

The next step is to clamp the cord. I hold my hand out expecting Doug to hand me the cord clamps, but again he tries to give me the scalpel. "Don't you think we should clamp the cord before we cut it?" I say quietly.

"Oh yea!" he says, digging into the kit again. He quickly produces the clamps and I measure about 6 inches from the baby and attach the first clamp and then attach the second one two more inches away.

Turning to Doug and holding out my hand for the third time I say, "Now, you can give me the scalpel."

True to form, instead of anticipating what I need he has to dig into the kit again to find it. I cut the cord and wrap the baby in a disposable blanket.

Now that the baby is taken care of and appears to be normal, I turn my attention to the mother. When I attempt to hand the baby to her she throws her hands over her eyes and says she doesn't want to see or hold it. Her sister, who had been holding her hand and comforting her throughout the delivery, starts to argue with her sister.

"You do to want this baby," she says.

The mother still holding her hands over her eyes says, "No, I don't."

This argument goes back and forth for a minute or two with the mother dramatically holding her hands over her eyes the whole time. I quickly realize the mother is serious about not wanting to see her new baby. I finally stop the argument by telling them this can be settled later. I then hand the baby to its Aunt. It is apparent she loves and wants her.

At first I think the mother's reaction is because she is afraid that the baby might not be healthy. I attempt to reassure her that the baby seems to be fit as a fiddle and normal in every way.

"I don't care," she shouts, "I don't want it. I don't want to see it."

"Do you have any other children?" I ask.

I see pictures of two different children in the house and assume they are hers. She tells me that she does indeed have two children. I had hoped that by reminding her of her other kids she would change her mind but it doesn't work.

While my partner takes vitals I take the sister off to the side and ask her if she knows why her sister is acting like this. The sister explains, "It's because the daddy up and died a little while ago. She's afraid the baby will remind her of him."

This explanation didn't exactly make sense to me. I do know that the normal excitement and good feeling I usually have delivering a baby was greatly reduced.

When we arrive at the hospital, the sister is still holding the baby and Mom is still holding her hands over her eyes. After getting the patient and baby to the O.B. department, I call the social worker and explain what had happened hoping she would be able to help in some way. I hope she did.

Is it Over Yet?

Its early evening, its cold, it's raining, it's about a week before Christmas, and last thing my partner and I want to do is make an 80 mile trip to Houston. Dispatch has just informed me we have an emergency transfer from the labor delivery at Doctors hospital to Herman hospital in downtown Houston. "Hey Debbie get your travelin' shoes on. We've got a 15 year old they say is in premature labor, going to Herman."

Debbie, ever the optimist, starts to chant, "we're going to deliver a baybee!"

"No we're not," I tell her, "You know good and well most of the O.B. patients we transport are nowhere near having their baby. The hospital just says they're emergencies so the ambulance will hurry up and get the patient out of their way."

We walk into the labor and delivery department and I spot the doctor sitting at a small desk writing notes.

"Well doc, are we going to deliver this one?" I ask jokingly.

"No way, it's her first child. Labor pains are 10 minutes apart and she's only dilated 4 centimeters. You'll have plenty of time."

"Sounds good to me. What room is she in?" I ask.

The nurse gives me a report as we walk down the hall. "She is 15 years old in active labor with contractions about 10 minutes apart. She is about two months early so we want to get her downtown so they will be able to take care of the baby. It's her first so you'll have plenty of time."

I have now had two people in a matter of a minute or so tell me, "Plenty of time." We enter the patient's room just as a contraction starts. The nurse impatiently waits for it to stop then hurries to get her unhooked from the various monitors. Meanwhile Debbie and I get the stretcher ready and park it alongside the bed.

Contraction over, the nurse quickly helps the patient move to the stretcher. As we head down the hall I tell the nurse, "If I didn't know better I'd think you' all were trying to get us out of here before she has this baby."

In the most professional tone she can muster the nurse tells us, "Nonsense, we just want her to get downtown before it gets too late. You'll have plenty of time. Her parents are already on the way and her aunt will be riding with you."

We take off down the hall to the ambulance dock, about a 3 or 4 minute walk. As we lift the patient into the ambulance another contraction starts.

"You know Debbie, I may just be a dumb country paramedic but I'm willing to swear those last two contractions were only three or four minutes apart. I think we've been had."

"Wouldn't be the first time," Debbie replies.

She's right. It's not uncommon for a hospital to lie to the receiving hospital and the ambulance about the condition of a patient so they can as it is called "dump the patient." Dumping is when a hospital wants to get rid of a patient for various reasons. No insurance is the most common one. Not wanting to have the liability of taking care of a critical patient or premature baby is another. As a result they stretch the truth and in some cases lie about the condition of the patient. In this case the receiving hospital probably wouldn't agree to let the patient be transported if they knew a baby that is supposed to be premature might be delivered before arrival at their facility.

"Let's get going and make it quick," I tell Debbie.

As she reaches for the switch to turn on the emergency lights Debbie asks, "Do you want me to code it down there?"

"No just get us down there. I will let you know if we need to run with the lights on. It could just be a coincidence that the last two contractions were that close together."

I knew better. I also knew that I really didn't want to deliver a premature baby with all the possible complications that would create.

The aunt jumps in the front passenger seat and in a few seconds we are heading to Houston.

"Here we go," I say to the patient who is scared to death.

Who would blame her? She's 15, in active labor, in an ambulance with 2 total strangers, and it's her first kid.

I just have time to take the patients vital signs and hook her up on the heart monitor when another contraction starts. I look at my watch. It has only been three minutes since the last contraction. During the contraction she tells me she feels like she has to push. Great, I think. I am now convinced that I will be delivering a baby before we get to the receiving hospital.

"Debbie go ahead and turn on the lights. She just had another contraction."

Debbie flips the switches and I feel the unit pick up speed.

We are on the freeway now, so I know that if we hurry we can make it to the other hospital in about an hour. Yep, I think to myself we'll be delivering this one in just a few minutes Contractions quickly jump from three minutes apart to less than two lasting for over a minute. I quickly think about the various hospitals we will pass on the way to Houston that could take care of a premature baby. My conclusion is that any of them would be better than the back of an ambulance.

I know that the most important thing in caring for a preemie is airway. I had never intubated a premature baby, heck I had never intubated a baby at all at that point in my career. I start to get somewhat apprehensive at the prospect.

Another contraction and the patient yells, "Something happened, something happening, I'm all wet down there."

I can see amniotic fluid running off my stretcher. The patient is yelling due to the contraction and just being scared. I try to calm her down but don't make much progress. I check the patient and can see the top of the baby's head.

"Pull over!" I tell Debbie. "Find a place to get off the freeway and make it quick."

"Alright, we're going to deliver a baby!"

She picks up the microphone and informs the dispatcher that we are pulling over to deliver the baby. The dispatcher acknowledges and wishes us good luck. That's good, because we'll need it if the baby has any complications.

As we exit the freeway and enter a parking lot at strip center, I open the O.B. kit and put on the gloves. Debbie has stopped and is quickly in the back to help.

"Get the intubation kit out just in case he has any breathing problems," I tell Debbie, "Contractions ten minutes apart, you'll have plenty of time… yea right," I say to no one in particular.

One more contraction and the head is out and to my surprise the baby is starting to breath. I grab the bulb syringe and suction its nose and mouth. One last contraction and the baby is born.

I do a quick assessment called an APGAR rating, APGAR is a mnemonic to help medical personnel gage how good or bad a newborn baby is doing. A stands for appearance, the color of the skin, P is pulse or heart rate. G is grimace or reflex irritability. A stands for activity or muscle tone, R is respirations, or how may time a minute the baby is breathing. Using this standard newborns are rated on a scale of 1, barely alive, to perfect 10, with each category getting number rating of zero, one, or two. For example, no pulse would be a 0, a pulse below 100 is a score of 2 and if the pulse if over 100 beats per minute the score is 3. No baby is a ten just after birth. A seven or eight is considered very good. I give him a rating of seven.

"Well what do you think Debbie darn good looking for a baby that was supposed to be 2 months premature?"

Happy that the baby is breathing on its own and doing well, I breathe a sigh of relief. I wrap him up and present him to his confused and overwhelmed mother.

Debbie grabs the microphone and radios dispatch that we have delivered the baby and that mother and child are doing well. The dispatcher congratulates us over the air, about the only time they get to say it is when a baby is born or we resuscitate a full arrest.

"Debbie, just for fun, ask them to call L&D at the hospital and let them know when and where we delivered the baby. They should get a kick out of knowing their watches run slower than ours."

We found out later that from the time we radioed we were pulling over until Debbie told them we had delivered the baby was only eight minutes. One of the fastest delivers I have ever seen considering just 30 minutes prior the labor pains were 10 minutes apart.

"Plenty of time... Yea right!"

Chapter 2….A Funny Thing Happened

As a paramedic I strived to be sympathetic toward all of my patients. Sometimes the circumstances that caused the injury were amusing to me and my partners. I always tried to treat my patients with respect due to them. I also tried to set a lighter mood when I thought it was appropriate. Other times comments made by patients or others involved in the incident were amusing. Others were amusing due to the attitude and actions of the patient and bystanders. Many times the patient just did something stupid, I mean even more stupid than everyday stupid calls. Don't get me wrong we all do dumb and or stupid things; most of the time we don't get hurt or if we do it is a minor injury and we don't call for medical attention. Read on and see what I am talking about.

A young mother in a panic because her baby has swallowed a mouthful of shampoo needs to be reassured that her baby is not in any real danger. I have changed a scene like this from one of a near hysteria to smiles and giggles by telling the mother she is going to need extra diapers. When she asks why I told her shampoo makes a great laxative. It was my way of letting her know things weren't nearly as serious as she thought they were.

A Free Trip to Jail

Keith is driving, as we round the corner on to Timber Mill road. Since its early afternoon on a week day there shouldn't be any problem finding it. I quickly spot the house and tell Keith. "Ok, Keith this is it, 3515," I say pointing to a two story contemporary style home. Keith comes to a stop on the street in front of the house. Even experienced drivers can have difficulty backing out of a narrow driveway filled with tricycles, cars, and kids. The cops don't like us blocking the road but there is little they can do about it.

Even though he has only worked in EMS for about a month, Keith is one of those people you know will probably become a good paramedic. Tall, skinny, and sporting a crew cut he looks like a lot of other young men in this line of work but that is where the similarity ended. A lot of people his age are always in emergency mode, that is always hyped up and ready for the big crash. Keith is a laid back country boy that usually rolls with the punches.

I grab the jump kit while Keith gets the oxygen bag. We cautiously approach the door, knock and instinctively step back. While neither I any other paramedic I know has ever been shot at through a door, we all act as if it could happen. Even though the call is supposed to be an overdose you never know what you are walking into.

In a perfect world an officer would have arrived on the scene and made sure the coast was clear before we entered the house. In the real world we would often arrived before the deputies and used our own judgment about waiting for them.

After a few moments the door is slowly opened by a middle aged woman wearing a beige terry cloth bath robe. Dark streaks under her eyes indicate a mixture of tears and mascara. She is holding a half empty bottle of vodka in her free hand.

"Who the hell called you?" She screams, obviously angry, "That no good cheating son of a b---- husband of mine did it, didn't he?"

"We don't know who called. We were told someone needed help here," I figured it wouldn't be a good idea to use the word overdose since she was already angry and drunk.

Keith quickly picks up on this and tries to get her confidence, "Mam, could we please come in and make sure you're OK?"

"I don't give a f--- what you do," With that said she lets go of the door, walks back into the house and sits down in an arm chair.

Keith and I look at each other with a "what the heck is going on" look and follow her into the house. As Keith and I approach she scoops several pills off the end table throws them in her mouth and swallows them aided by several gulps of vodka.

"What are you doing?" Demands Keith. He is standing in front of her now and grabs for the vodka.

"Leave me the f--- alone!" She says, dramatically pulling the bottle out of his reach.

Now that she has an audience she tries to grab more of the pills scattered across the table. Determined to take control of the situation Keith pushes the pills out of her reach. "Get out of my way you little bastard!" she yells. Trying unsuccessfully to reach around him she falls back into the chair.

Keith, trying to catch her off guard, makes another grab for the booze. This time she hides it behind her back. "I told you you little s--- to leave me the f--- alone!"

Having been through this many times with other patients in the same state of mind, I realize she is going to need time to calm down before we can start to deal with her. Keith on the other hand is determined to take control of the situation. Seeing he's not getting anywhere using the aggressive approach he decides to change tactics.

When she answered the door Keith and I had noticed what appeared to be superficial cuts on her neck. They were more scratches than cuts but Keith decides he will try to draw her attention away from the pills and vodka by addressing the cuts. "Mam, can I at least look at the cuts on your neck?" he asks in his kindest voice as he bends down to see. Finding it hard to see since the curtains are drawn and no lights are on he grabs a small flashlight out of the trauma kit. He turns it on and shines it on her neck. She lifts her head and for a moment and appears to be cooperating.

"You want to see? Here take a good look!" With that said she grabs her robe with both hands and yanks it open exposing her breast. "You wanted to see them you little pervert take a look."

I am extremely surprised by this action but not nearly as much as Keith. He turns beet red, drops the light, and stumbles back several steps before regaining some of his composure. "No, no that's, that's OK." He stutters.

The patient who is, by the way, a fairly attractive 42 year old seeing she has gotten the response she wanted from her little show continues the insults. "What's the matter little boy scared of a real woman?"

Seeing I need to step in and attempt to get control of the situation, I tell Keith to check the open pill bottle on the table to see what she's taking.

"It's Valium," He tells me.

"Pick up what is left on the table so she can't get to them," he nods and starts picking them up and putting them in the bottle.

"Leave those alone you little b------, they're mine!" she demands as she tries to get up and grab the bottle out of Keith's hand. Drunk and under the influence of an unknown quantity of

Valium she stumbles and falls back into the chair. In the brief moment she is out of the chair I see my chance and grab the vodka bottle she had hidden behind her.

"You can't do that you fat son of a b---- it belongs to me."

"No," I tell her, "You are not getting the booze or the pills back. You are going to calm down and let us take you to the hospital. Do you understand?" I ask.

"You m----- f------ aren't taking me anywhere. Leave me the f--- alone."

I hear a car pull into the driveway and ask Keith to see who it is. He goes to the door and quickly informs me it's the deputy. In a few moments he's in the living room wanting to know what's going on. I quickly tell him what little we know and that the patient is refusing to let us treat her. While I brief the deputy our patient finally makes it to her feet. Stumbling around the living room she continues to insult us.

Being a highly trained deputy from rural Texas he sets out to show us how to handle a woman. Getting face to face with her he uses the tried and true line that most cops use in this situation. "Either you go with the ambulance or you go to jail," he says.

"Take my ass to jail. I don't care what the f---- you do. You gun totin red neck pig."

Keith turns to me and whispers sarcastically, "Yea, that worked. Guess he showed us."

It's true that most of the time when faced with hospital or jail even the drunkest patient will choose the hospital. This is one of the times when the patient truly didn't care. Having used his best line the deputy repeats the choices to the patient. Again, in no uncertain terms she refuses ambulance transport.

At this point the deputy steps back to where we are standing, "What a mouth!" He exclaims.

"Aren't you going to arrest her?" I ask him in the most sincere voice I can muster knowing he didn't have any real reason to take her in.

"Can't, she hasn't done anything to take her in for," he says, confirming what I already know.

Another car screeches to a halt outside. *Now what!* I think. Moments later her husband burst through the front door. Seeing him unleashes the worst string of profanity we have heard yet. After all was said and done she was accusing him of cheating on her.

The husband, who is best described as the pretty boy type, only half heartedly attempts to deny any wrong doing. Custom suit, over styled hair, dark tan, and too much gold jewelry made him look like a poster child for slick operators.

"What did she take this time?" he asked.

"She was drinking vodka and taking Valium when we got here. We took them away from her but she has refused to tell us how many she's taken."

"Take her to the hospital so they can pump her stomach or something," he says.

"If you can convince her to go I will be glad to. So far she's refused to let us treat her," I tell him over her constant screams telling him to get out of the house.

"I don't care what she says damn it. Take her to the g-- d— hospital," he demands.

"She's still conscious and aware of what's going on. I can't force her to go."

The husband then turns to the deputy, "Take her ass to jail then. I don't care where she goes just get her out of here."

I see the husband has the same vulgar vocabulary as his wife.

"Can't, she hasn't done anything illegal," the deputy informs him.

Hearing her husband tell the deputy to take her to jail puts her over the edge. "Get out of my house you cheating bastard. All of you get your asses out of my house," she screams.

I am now totally fed up with her and slick Willie, "Keith, get the kit we're out of here."

Not wanting to be left in the house with a screaming cussing drunk, the husband and deputy also head for the front door. Once outside we stop to evaluate the situation. I am about to suggest calling someone she trust to talk to her when she opens the front door.

"I told you bastards to get the f--- out of here," taking a step out the door she raises her right hand above her head and throws a large butcher knife in our general direction. The knife falls harmlessly to the ground a few feet from where we are standing.

The deputy looks at the knife then at the patient and says, "that's attempted assault on a police officer. Now I have a reason to take her in," he starts moving toward her reaching for his handcuffs.

The patient, still standing just outside the door, realizes she has now gone too far and turns to run back in the house. The deputy moving more quickly than I have ever seen takes several steps and reaches her before she can get the door closed. Taking her by surprise he manages to get the cuffs on one wrist. At that moment the fighting and cussing was on. With her free arm she swings around and starts hitting the deputy in the face.

"Let go of me you little bastard he's the one you should arrest he's the one that f----s every woman he meets."

Even though her blows aren't really causing any damage the deputy is having difficulty getting her under control. Fighting the urge to see the outcome of a wrestling match between a deputy and a mad drunk woman in a bathrobe, I step in and give him a hand. She was concentrating on hitting him and didn't see me when I grabbed her free hand and brought it up behind her so he could finish cuffing her. The deputy immediately starts wrestling her toward the patrol car. Still putting up a fight but finally wearing down she continues to cuss and scream even after being put in the back seat.

During this skirmish her husband stands nearby with his arms folded not saying or doing anything. After watching his wife being arrested the husband goes into the house and closes the door without saying a word.

The deputy heads for jail with his cargo still cussing and screaming.

Do You See the Blood?

A five year old boy is carried into his house by his father after being hit by a car. The boy had done what we were all warned not to do as children. Which is, run out into the street after a ball? Luckily for him the car almost stopped before knocking him down.

I had only been told that a child had been hit by a car. Like most paramedics I always got a bit more anxious when a kid was involved. As we get near the house I expect to see a crowd gathered around a moaning child lying in the middle of the street. To my surprise I only see an older child in the front yard flagging us down.

"Where's the patient?" I ask, as I jump out of the ambulance.

"In the living room, Dad carried him in," he replies.

Great! I think, *pick him up carry him in so he can be comfy.* People often forget about making patients injuries worse by moving them.

I walk into the house and see a small boy lying in the middle of the living room floor. As usual I start looking for injuries as I approach the patient. I spot several abrasions on his legs but except for some minor bleeding they don't look serious. He is conscious and doesn't appear to have any obvious fractures.

Kneeling down next to him I ask the question I ask every conscious trauma patient, "Where does it hurt?"

In a very serious tone he looks at me and asks, "Do you see the blood?"

"Yes," I answer.

"That's where it hurts."

This boy's logic certainly makes sense to me. After being checked out at the hospital, his only injuries were the abrasions.

I've Been Shot! No You Haven't!

It's about ten o'clock at night when we arrive at the local bowling alley. It's hot and humid a typical summer night in Texas. I spot three young men standing in the parking lot waving at us.

"What do you bet they are the ones looking for an ambulance?" I tell my partner.

I get out of the unit and can hear one of the men yelling, "He's been shot! Hurry up!"

I make a quick survey to see which one appears to be shot. All are standing, there is no obvious external bleeding, and no one appears to be in any great distress.

"Ok, I give up which one of you got shot?" I ask.

"I did. I did," shouts one of the young men. He is tall, skinny, wearing baggy pants, and a loose fitting tee shirt.

"Where did you get hit? Where do you hurt?" I question him as I am able to get a closer look now that I know which one got shot, I still don't see any obvious wounds.

"I don't know man. I just know they shot me," he answers as he starts grabbing his chest and abdomen.

"OK calm down. Let us check you out."

While people who have been shot don't always know exactly where or how many times they have been shot, they usually have a rough idea. This man doesn't seem to have a clue. Since he is grabbing at his chest and abdomen I lift his shirt to take a look. My partner holds a flashlight while I carefully inspect the patient for any signs of a bullet wound. I don't see any obvious wounds but my exam is hampered by the man continuing to grab at his chest and abdomen.

"I can't believe they shot me man," he keeps saying.

"I don't see anything. Do you?" I ask turning to my partner.

"I don't see anything either," he says.

I look the patient in the eye in an attempt to get his attention, "Listen to me. You haven't been shot. I don't see any signs of a bullet wound," I tell him, "If you would try to calm down for a minute you'll see you don't hurt anywhere."

'That's easy for you to say man. You aren't the one who's been shot," he says in a panic.

I am now about fed up with him. I realize I need to get more forceful to get his attention. I finally manage to grab his arms which are flailing wildly. I can smell the beer on his breath and with him being as hyper as he is there is no telling what else he is on.

"Did you see a gun? Did you see who did it?" I ask him trying to redirect his attention.

"I don't know man. I didn't see anything they just drove by and shot me," he screams.

I have now officially had enough of him acting like an idiot. I turn my attention to the other two young men who are standing around.

"Are you his friends or what?"

One finally speaks up; he is also tall and skinny and for the most part looks pretty much like the one that claims he's been shot,. "Yea, man we hang together."

"Did you actually see anyone shoot at him? Or do you just think they did?"

"Man I don't know. I heard a pop and he started yellin he'd been shot."

"So I don't suppose you saw anything either?" I say turning to the third young man in the group. He immediately cops an attitude.

"Hey man you need to worry about taking care of him instead of hassling us."

"You listen to me and listen good. He has not been shot. YOU three need to go home and sober up from whatever it is you're on and quit wasting my time. I'm leaving. Now if you want to hang around and keep screaming you've been shot that's OK with me, but I'm leaving." With that said my partner and I pick up our equipment and head for the ambulance. A deputy I know quite well arrives just as I finish my speech.

"Hey, Ramsey what did they do to piss you off?" he asked.

I give him a quick rundown of the situation with the man claiming he's been shot still yelling at us to do something.

"I'll take care of it," the deputy tells us.

By the time it was all over the "man who had been shot" had been arrested for possession of amphetamines. I understand he screamed all night that he had been shot. I guess the paranoia that comes with taking "speed" was working overtime that night.

Water Water Everywhere Not a Drop to Drink

It's Saturday night about two in the morning and the last thing I wanted to do was check out a drunk that had been arrested for DWI at the county jail. Unfortunately paramedics rarely get to do what they really wanted to do while on shift, that is, sleep all night.

Craig the jailer is escorting Jason and me through the maze of halls and steel doors that lead back to the cell occupied by our patient. "They brought him in about an hour ago. He started complaining of chest pain after we locked him up. Says he has a bad heart. He's so drunk he can't tell us anything else."

We finally stop and Craig puts the oversize key into the lock and turns it. He yanks on the handle and opens the solid steel door. The only openings in it are a small slot about waist high that's for taking a food trays in and out and a small door at eye level for looking in on the prisoner. Just inside the door to the right is a small aluminum sink that is attached to the wall. Just beyond that is an aluminum commode. Along the same wall are bunk beds. Big steel plates welded to the wall with a 2 inch mattress and no sheets. There is just enough room to get between edge of the bed and the opposite wall. The patient is laying on his right side in the bottom bunk. He struggles to sit up as I kneel down. Just one look and I can tell he is a long time drinker. Bone thin, gray skin color, sunken cheeks, all too common characteristics I have seen over the years. Propping himself up with one arm he tries to focus on me.

"Whathehellyouwant?" he asked, his speech so slurred the words run together. The smell of beer and cigarettes on his breath are almost nauseating.

"I'm a paramedic. They told me you were having chest pain."

"Leavemealoneyoufatsob! Idon'tneedanyhelpfromyou."

Since our uniforms are similar to police uniforms I figure he thinks I'm a cop. "Listen to me. I'm not a cop. I'm a paramedic with the ambulance. The jailer called me and said you were having chest pain," then real slowly I ask, "Are you having chest pain?"

"Anitoldyoutoleavemealoneyoufatbastard." As he says this he doubles up his fist as if he's going to hit me. Now remember he is still holding himself up with the other arm. In the same moment the jailer seeing what he is doing moves in and pins him face down in the mattress. I had instinctively moved back but knew he probably couldn't have swung without falling over.

"Letmeupyoupig," cries the drunk. It seems he does know the difference between me and the jailer.

Craig has the prisoner in an arm lock with his face buried in the mattress. "Are you going to let the medics treat you or not?" he asks.

"Itolyouldon'tneedanyhelpfromthatfatsob. Nowleavemealone."

"Third times a charm," I say as I stand up. "Looks like he's refusing treatment," Jason and I start making our way out of the cell.

Craig lets go of him and is following us out of the cell. The drunk struggles to sit up but can't make it. He hollers at us, "Ineedadrinkofwater. Getmeadrinkofwaterdamit."

"I'll get you some water later," replies Craig.

"Iwantsomewaternow!" he shouts.

"And I told you I'll get it later. Now shut up."

He is lying with his head at the end of the bunk next to the toilet. He then does one of the most disgusting things I have ever seen; he dips his cupped hand into water in the toilet. Jason says what the rest of us are thinking. "He's not going to do what I think he going to do is he?" With that said he brings up a small quantity of toilet water and laps it up out of his hand.

"Well that's about the grossest thing I've seen in a long time," says Craig, as we all nod in agreement.

"And they say alcohol impairs your judgment, hogwash," I say sarcastically.

Craig kicks the door shut just as the prisoner makes another dip into the toilet.

Mini Gang Fight

It's hot, it's humid, it's ten o'clock at night, and it's a typical summer night in Southeast Texas. Jason and I have been running calls all day long and are tired, hungry, and sweaty. Meanwhile across town, Juanita is celebrating her 16th birthday in her parents' back yard. Her boyfriend, Jose, and the rest of the gang are helping her celebrate.

Several members of a rival gang, actually the only other gang in town, jump the fence and with knives drawn run through the party crowd. In the few seconds it takes for them to run to the other side of the yard and make their escape they have inflicted several knife wounds on the party goers.

Jason and I arrive on the scene thinking we are responding to a medical call. We are, to say the least, surprised to find several people sitting and standing in the back yard holding towels, napkins, and various other absorbent materials to cuts. Apparently in an effort to keep the cops out of the picture they told the dispatcher someone was sick when they called 911.

Just as I start to wonder why the police haven't been dispatched to this the scene the radio springs to life, "Medic 5 Navasota."

"Go ahead Medic 5."

"You might want to get a unit over here. It appears we have several people with knife wounds at this location."

As soon as I let go of the transmit button I hear 2 units head our way. The Navasota officers were always good at helping us out when we asked.

"We don't need no cops here man," A young man tells us as he gets up from the picnic table holding a paper towel to his forearm.

Jason wanting to stop anyone from doing something stupid immediately starts to take control of the scene. He points to the young man who is attempting to act tough in front of his peers, "You, sit back down and keep quiet."

The young man reluctantly sits back down.

"You can't talk to him like that," Comments a female in the crowd.

"We can and will talk to you like that. You lied about what happened hoping the cops won't show up and when the people who are going to help you show up you act like you are going to jump us. I don't think so," I tell the crowd. By this time I have counted five or six people who seem to be wounded. No one is lying on the ground, so I am relieved that everyone appears to have non-life threatening injuries.

"Now that we understand each other you want to tell us what happened?" asked Jason as he points to the kid that started to get up when we first arrived. He quickly tells us about the sneak attack as I make my way to the picnic table to set up a triage center.

"Ok here's the deal. Everyone who got cut come over here so we can check you out," I tell them. The mother of the girl having the party gets up from her lawn chair holding a bloody towel to her left forearm. Her daughter also has a cut to her forearm but it is not very serious. Two other teenage boys' one with a cut to his upper arm and the other with a superficial cut to his back head toward the table.

"You want to call for another unit or not?" Jason asked as we check out our patients.

"It will take them 30 minutes to get here and they're all walking wounded let's just load them up. We're only a mile or so from the hospital."

"You're the boss."

"You better believe it," I say smugly.

"Hey, everyone who wants to go to the hospital in the ambulance follow me," Jason tells them as we walk to the front yard.

The cops have arrived and are getting the story of what happened from several of the non-injured people in the crowd. As usual with gang related violence no one could give them a description of the people who did the cutting.

Everyone finds a place to sit in the back of the unit. Because we are so close to the hospital I decided to not worry about getting names and information until we get there. Jason has just enough time to call the emergency room on the cell phone and warn them we are coming in with several patients with minor injuries. Just as he dials the number he hollers back through the walk way wanting to know how many patients we actually do have.

"Six," I tell him.

"Six. I thought we had five at the scene."

"Well, there are six now."

"Ok,"

I realize he's right. We only checked out five people back at the house. I quickly look around and see an extra young man sitting on the squad bench. I don't remember examining him at the scene and don't see any wounds.

"Hey you, what's wrong with you?" I ask pointing to him.

"There ain't nothing wrong with me man," he replies quietly.

"Then why are you going to the hospital?" I ask.

"I don't know. You told everyone to get into the ambulance so I got in."

"I told everyone who was injured to get in the ambulance. Why would you go to the hospital if you weren't injured?"

He just shrugs his shoulders and looks at the floor without answering. Great! I think, now I'll have to write a report on him. Maybe I can put the chief complaint as stupidity.

I head into the emergency room followed by my entourage. "You sit over there," I tell the uninjured boy. Pointing to the seats reserved for family members.

"What's wrong with him?" The nurse asks.

"Absolutely nothing."

"Then why did he come in?"

"Well it seems when I told everyone who was injured to get in the ambulance he didn't hear the part about being injured."

"But, that doesn't make any sense," replies the nurse somewhat confused.

"No, it doesn't."

Chapter 3….Gun Shot Wounds

Because of the influence of movies, TV, and in many cases people talking about something they have no real knowledge of you develop a preconceived notion of things that you later learn are false. What happens when a person is shot is probably one of the most misunderstood events that come to mind. Before I became a paramedic I thought when you got shot you died. Actually more people survive than die from them. Even people shot in the head will sometimes survive for several hours or even days. Some even live to tell about it. It is really amazing how the human body fights to live.

Merry Christmas

It's a week before Christmas a father and his son are unloading their truck after deer hunting. The father goes into the house and before he gets back out for the next load he hears a shot. Not knowing what has happened he runs outside to find his 21 year old son lying in the street at the back of the truck. He sees blood coming from his head and calls for the ambulance.

"Medic 7 respond to a shooting at 731 Elm." the dispatcher says.

David and I look at each other as we head to the ambulance. We know the address is in an upper middle class neighborhood, an area we don't normally get calls for shootings. It's not that well-to-do people don't shoot each other but it isn't a normal occurrence.

I grab for the microphone and radio the dispatcher. "Medic 9 is enroute to the call on Elm Street. Has law enforcement been notified?" I ask.

Logic would dictate that if you were a dispatcher you would automatically notify the police whenever there's a call that involves guns. It's somewhat disconcerting to round the corner of a potentially dangerous call and not see a deputy.

"Medic 9 this is reported as an accidental shooting. Do you think you will need them?" the dispatcher asks.

"Yes, we need them. Also do you have any information as to how many people are wounded and what happened?" I ask.

"Medic 9, only information available is it's an accidental shooting. I will get law enforcement to respond."

Going to a call and having little or no idea as to what we are getting into is fairly common. One service I worked for even had a policy of not telling the ambulances any details of what they were going to even if the dispatcher knew. The logic behind this bright idea was that if the ambulance crews were told too much they might get a preconceived idea of what they were getting into and possibility affect their treatment of the patient.

To be honest there are many factors that may prevent a dispatcher from getting and or relaying enough information to the EMS crews. One is that sometimes when people call 911 they are so excited just getting an address is extremely difficult. Another is being too busy to get enough information. If you are the only dispatcher and have several calls going on at one time you may not be able to get full details.

Conflicts between EMS crews and some dispatchers have been around since and probably before I got started in EMS over 35 years ago and is still going strong.

"Well I shouldn't have wasted my breath asking for more information," I say.

"You know how some of them are. Why do you bother?" David asks.

"I can dream can't I? Maybe someday they will get tired of me asking for more information and actually give it just to shut me up."

"Yea, and someday there will be world peace." David says sarcastically.

We know it is going to take us about 10 minutes to get to the call so we hope that the cops are there when we get there. Moments later one of our first responders that dispatch forgot to send on the call goes on location. He was only a few blocks away when he heard the call go out on his scanner. He made an executive decision to go anyway. About a minute passes and he comes on the radio to tell us what has happened.

"1124 to Medic 9," he calls.

"Medic 9 go ahead," I answer.

"Medic 9 you have a 21 year old male with a severe gunshot wound to the head. He's still breathing and has a heartbeat," he tells us.

"That's clear 1124 we will be there in 5 to 6 minutes."

David and I quickly make the decision to put Lifeflight on standby. There are two reasons for this decision. The hospital that Lifeflight flies out of has a level one trauma center. If the patient has any chance of survival it will be the best place for him.

Another consideration on a call of this nature is the possibility of a patient being an organ donor. It sounds cruel to some people for paramedics to be thinking about a person being an organ donor but you have to be realistic. A young person shot in the head that still has a heartbeat is a perfect candidate for organ donation.

Just prior to our arrival on the scene dispatch confirms that Lifeflight is on standby. That means the pilot and crew are sitting in the helicopter waiting for the word to go or not.

As we round the corner I can see the first responder attending to the patient. He is lying on the edge of the grass next to the street. There are also two deputies on the scene.

David goes to check the patient and I grab the kits. Moments later I kneel down next to the patient and quickly notice the entrance wound above his right eye just below the hair line. There is a large bandage called a multi-trauma dressing laying under the back his head. It's soaked with a combination of blood and brains. The first responder tells me that the exit wound is in the very back of the patient's head and it is about 2 to 3 inches in diameter.

"Are there any other wounds?" I ask.

"I don't think so but I have been so busy attending to his head wound I haven't had time to check real close," he says.

While David gets ready to intubate the patient, I look up at the deputy and tell him to get Lifeflight heading our way. I then start a head to toe assessment to see if there are any other injuries or bullet wounds. I don't find any. What I do notice is no family members are around. The deputy makes a quick call on the radio and I hear the dispatcher tell him Lifeflight is on the way with an E.T.A. of 20 minutes.

David is now ready to intubate the patient. He puts the laryngoscope into the patient's mouth and lifts his tongue out of the way with the blade. On the end of the metal blade is a small light bulb that lights up the patient's throat. The object is to visualize the patient's vocal cords using the light and pass the endotracheal tube between them past the larynx into the patient's trachea. This lets the paramedic have complete control of the airway.

David gets the tube in place and I check for lung sounds to confirm placement. This is done by listening to make sure you hear air go into the lungs when you ventilate the patient and not into their stomach. If you get the tube into the esophagus you ruin any chance the patient might have had. It's a 50 /50 chance of getting it right but since the path of least resistance is into the esophagus the E.T. tube will go there if you don't watch what you are doing.

I establish an IV in the patient's left forearm. We then begin the task of packaging him for transport. Since we still haven't found out what really happened to the patient other than being shot we assume that he also fell. That means full cervical spine immobilization in addition to all of the other treatment he is receiving. The multi-trauma dressing that was put under his head by the first responder is now completely soaked with blood and brains. Since the brain is not a muscle it falls apart pretty easy when it is damaged. What ends up happening especially in a shooting is the brain is literally scrambled and you end up with little bits of grayish matter mixed with the blood. The first time you see this it takes a few seconds to realize what you are seeing. It also hits you that everything that person was now is in little bits and pieces. It is also amazing as to how hard the human body attempts to stay alive. In the case of this young man a large portion

57

of his brain is lying on the ground and on the bandage but his heart continues to beat.

We get a few rolls of bandages out and wrap them around his head along with the trauma dressing that is already there. It's a feeble attempt to keep more blood and brain from leaking out of the 3 inch wound in the back of his head.

As we place the patient on a back board the deputy approaches us with some more information. "The fire department is going to land Lifeflight in the Kroger parking lot. Dispatch says Lifeflight is 15 minutes away. Oh, by the way, the boy's father says him and his son had just gotten back from a hunting trip. He says they were unpacking the back of the truck and he had just gone into the house when he heard a shot. Says he ran outside to find him lying in the street with several rifles and a pistol lying on the ground beside him. He thinks his son must have tripped or fallen as he stepped out of the back of the truck causing him to drop the guns. He thinks one of them went off when it hit the ground."

"Where are the guns then? And why isn't anyone from the family out here?" I ask.

"We thought it was kinda funny that the guns were gone also. Dad says he didn't want his son to hurt himself anymore so he picked them up and took them into the house and hid them under the couch."

"Hid them under the couch, doesn't that sound a little strange to you?" I ask. I know people do strange things when they are excited but to me the idea of picking up the guns and carrying them into the house before you call for the ambulance seems ridiculous. Unfortunately I didn't have time to try to figure it out. We needed to get the patient into the ambulance and transport him the 6 blocks to parking lot before the helicopter lands.

As we load the patient into the unit I turn to the deputy and ask him if the family has been informed that their son is be flown to the hospital.

"No, not yet, they haven't asked," the deputy tells us.

"Since they aren't out here would you mind telling them we are getting ready to take him to the landing zone? By the way, do they have any idea of how bad he is?" The deputy doesn't answer me. He just nods his head and takes off into the house. I am starting to get frustrated at what I perceive to be strange actions by the patient's family and the deputy's lackadaisical attitude toward them. I can only imagine what any parent goes through when their child young or old is seriously injured, but I do know from experience most of them are concerned enough to be with their child inquiring as to his or her condition.

We are placing the patient into the ambulance when the father finally comes out of the house. "Can I see him before you take him?" he asks.

"Sure you can," I reply as I motion him into the back of the ambulance.

I know it may be the last time he will see his son alive. I try but can't imagine how he feels. Standing there looking at what was left of his son with a tube in his lungs and a hole the size of your fist in the back of his head he seems lost. He looks for a few seconds then ask us how to get to the hospital.

The first responder takes the father out of the ambulance to tell him how to get to the hospital. I swap the oxygen tubing from the portable tank to the large on board tank. We usually carry several small portable tanks to use while we are outside of the ambulance. When you are ventilating a patient the liter flow is set at 15 liters per minute it empties a portable tank fairly quickly so you hook up to the on board tank as soon as you can.

"You got it?" I ask David. He nods his head, signaling he is ready to go. Since he is already ventilating the patient I head to the front to make the quick drive to the parking lot.

I get out and see that the deputies have already left the scene. Don't want to miss the big helicopter landing. Some kids never grow up.

I get in the cab of the ambulance and head for the parking lot. I pull up next to the fire truck and of course the two deputies are already there. The firefighters picked a corner of the parking lot that is clear and have put out cones to signify the landing zone. I radio the dispatcher we are on location and waiting for Lifeflight. I switch to the mutual aid frequency on the radio. It is a frequency that all of the ambulances and fire departments in Southeast Texas use to talk to each other. Lifeflight also has the same frequency to make it easier to communicate with them.

I go back and help David while we wait for the helicopter. I spot the Assistant Chief and ask him to handle the communications. I knew he was already doing it but it is best to make sure.

I get into the back of the ambulance to help David with ventilating the patient. "How's he doing?" I ask.

"Holding on. Heart rate steady at 100. I'm surprised he's still with us," David says.

"So am I," I reply.

We had been with the patient for about 15 minutes. Due to the extent of his injuries both of us had expected him to die at anytime. The fact that his heart had continued to beat this long was just another testament of how the human body makes extraordinary efforts to live.

A large audience has gathered by the time Lifeflight lands. It doesn't take long for a crowd to form when people see a parking lot full of fire trucks, police cars, and an ambulance. Although they are staying back and behaving themselves it only takes one person trying to get a closer look to disrupt everything.

Even though I had radioed the crew of Lifeflight and had given them a patient assessment they are surprised when they finally lay eyes on him. "Now how big is the exit wound?" the doctor asks. Not believing that anyone could still have a heart beat with a hole the size of your fist in the back of his head.

I tell him again, "It is about 3 to 4 inches."

The doctor makes a quick assessment. He checks the patient's pupils and listens to lung sounds to make sure he is intubated properly. He finds both pupils completely dilated and fixed. He finds the ET tube in the proper place. We have an IV going so there isn't much left for the Lifeflight crew to do.

"What's his BP and heart rate?" the doctor asks.

"BP is 100/60; heart rate has been pretty much steady at 100," David tells him.

"Well, let's get him to the bird and get out of here before his heart quits. You've done everything that can be done for him," the doctor says shaking his head. He realizes it is just a matter of time.

I switch the oxygen back to the portable, put the heart monitor between his legs, and unhook the IVs from their hangers. A ritual that becomes automatic after a while. We get out of the back of the ambulance to find a crowd of at least 100 onlookers waiting to see something. I see a couple of flashes going off as we walk to the helicopter. Even though the patients head was wrapped up and there wasn't much of anything to see some people saw fit to record the incident.

The chopper lifts off and I have time to reflect on the call. In the end it really doesn't matter how or why the patient was shot. I feel it was probably an accident instead suicide because of the location of the entrance wound. Most people shoot themselves in the temple or in the mouth and on rare occasions behind the ear. The other possibility is that the father had something to do with it. He was the only other person in the general area, even though he claimed to be in the house at the time he heard the shot. He acted strange during the whole incident, but was it just his way of responding to a stressful situation or did he know more that he let on?

Catch Me if You Can

It's early Saturday morning and Theresa and I are washing the ambulance. We are at a sub-station in the southern section of our district. It is mainly a middle class suburban area and people are out early mowing lawns. When it's August in Southeast Texas, you get the outdoor chores done early if you're smart.

I'm handling the brush and Theresa is rinsing, like others in the neighborhood we are trying to get done before it gets too hot. We have just finished the left side and are dragging the hose, bucket, and truck brush to the other side when the pager starts to beep.

"Medic 7, "respond to a trauma call at 2431 Jimmy Lane."

"Oh well nothing like making a call in a half dirty unit," I say.

"You can look on the bright side and make the call in a half clean one," Theresa shoots back.

"I guess you're right. Just remember it will probably be close to 100 degrees by the time we get back and it will be your turn to wash."

Theresa has the motor started and I grab the microphone, "Medic 7 clear on the call at 2431 Jimmy Lane. Dispatch do you have any information as to the nature of the injury?" I ask this question knowing I will probably be told that no other information is available.

I am not disappointed when the dispatcher acknowledges me and tells us that the caller was too excited to give any information.

"Hope it's not a shooting," I say half joking half serious, "You know how I love surprises."

Actually that's one of the things that make EMS interesting, the surprises.

"Careful, you are going to jinx us," jokes Theresa.

She is referring to the long held superstition in EMS that if you talk about something it will happen. Actually it is more of an ongoing joke than a superstition. If you have had a slow day, you don't mention it because you will surely make calls the rest of the shift. You don't even dare say something to your partner like.

"Gee, it sure has been a long time since we had to go get Mr. Smith." Mr. Smith being the 400 pound diabetic that on a regular basis takes his insulin, forgets to eat supper, and goes in to insulin shock. Did I mention that Mr. Smith lives in a trailer on the side of a hill?

"It's the suburbs, don't you know people don't get shot in the suburbs," I joke back.

The address we were given was only about a mile away. Theresa turns the corner and we see someone flagging us down. The kid flagging us down is about 12 years old and very excited. As soon as we stop, he is running into the house.

"I'll get the kit," I tell Theresa as she radios dispatch we have arrived on the scene.

As we get near the front door, we can hear several people screaming.

"That doesn't sound good does it?' I ask rhetorically.

I enter the house and see the boy that flagged us down standing in the hall.

"In the back yard. he got shot," he tells me.

I turn to Theresa and say, "Told you so."

We immediately head through the house to the back door. As I get near the door I spot several small pools of blood on the floor that look like shoe prints. I look out and see a man and a woman kneeling on the patio. They are holding down a young boy with blood all over him.

The man, I learned later was the next door neighbor, is holding the boys leg in the air as blood runs out of the cowboy boot he's wearing. A woman obviously his mother kneels near him trying, without much luck, to calm the boy down. The boy is screaming and crying. His mother is doing the same and the man is attempting to stop the bleeding by squeezing the boy's calf.

I kneel next to them still not knowing how or why he was shot. A quick head to toe look does not reveal any other obvious wounds. He keeps screaming that his foot hurts, most of the time when children are screaming they will be ok. It's the ones that are whimpering and moaning that you really have to worry about.

I take the leg from the man and push on the pressure point behind the knee to see if this will stop the bleeding. It slows but blood is still running out of the boot. I remember seeing a doctor in the emergency room use a blood pressure cuff to stop bleeding long enough to bandage a wound. I turn to Theresa who is already opening trauma kit and ask her for the adult blood pressure cuff. She is confused for a second then realizes what I am about to do. I quickly wrap the cuff around the boy's thigh and pump it up until the bleeding stops. Ok, I think, now we have time to figure out what happened and make sure there are no other injuries.

"What happened?" I ask the mother.

Theresa talks to the boy in an attempt to calm him down while I do a head to toe exam to see if he has any other injures. As we do, the boy's mother who's starting to settle down now that we are on location is able to tell us how the shooting happened.

The boy had apparently found the 38 snub nose revolver kept under the pillow in the upstairs master bedroom. While playing with it, he had pulled the trigger shooting himself in the foot.

Mom is in the kitchen when she hears the shot. While she is trying to figure out what has happened, her son comes screaming down the stairs leaving a bloody trail as he runs into the back yard. Mom chases after him but the boy is in such a panic he won't stop. The next door neighbor out mowing his lawn seeing the commotion jumps the fence and tackles the boy.

I complete the exam and am relieved when I don't find any other injures. I grab my scissors and cut his boot off to see how badly he is wounded. As I pull the boot off the end of his blood soaked sock falls over making it look as if his toes have been shot off. Theresa and I are taken aback for a short moment until we realize the end of the sock is too flat to have toes in it. I carefully remove the sock to find the bullet has entered between his big and second toe and exited straight out the bottom of his foot. I was very relieved to see this.

"Well, Pilgrim," I tell the Mother and the boy in my best John Wayne voice, "it looks like a clean wound to me."

Even though no one laughs, I didn't really expect anyone to, it did lighten the mood. At least everyone had quit screaming.

To this day I can visualize the boy and his mother running circles in the back yard.

I can also just as easily see the boy dying or killing someone else that day. Just because someone thought it was smart to keep a loaded pistol under the pillow.

The Gift

One evening Debbie and I were just getting ready to eat supper when the pager went off. "Medic 9 respond to a shooting at the Downtown Hotel, PD on the scene."

The Downtown Hotel is an old run down two story building about a block from downtown Conroe, thus the name. It is also about a block from the Conroe Police Department. The main attraction of the hotel is a bar. I am sure it has something to do with the shooting.

We head to the hotel. Shortly before arrival one of the officers radios us.

"Medic 9 your patient will be sitting in my patrol car he has a gunshot wound to the back. He's still conscious and alert."

"Medic 9 received."

We pull into the parking lot to find 4 patrol cars. Mike, the officer that radioed us, points to his patrol car. The passenger side door is open and I see a heavy set gray haired man sitting in the seat.

"He doesn't look too bad from here," I say.

"Yea, but that one over there looks like he may have accidentally bumped his head getting into the patrol car," Debbie jokes as she puts the unit in park and turns off the emergency lights. One of my pet peeves is for emergency vehicles to keep their emergency lights on when it isn't necessary.

I look into the back seat of the other patrol car and see a medium build, middle aged man, who's face looks like it's taken a couple of good shots, "Yea, gotta learn to be careful."

We get out, grab the kit, and walk over to our patient.

"What happened?" I ask.

"That SOB shot me, that's what happened," he shouts pointing to the man in custody.

Our patient looks to be well over six feet tall and husky on top of that. For obvious reasons he is very upset.

"Where did he get you?" I ask, being more specific this time. I am next to him now and do a quick head to toe check. The only thing I can see is a small spot of blood on his upper right back.

"In my back over here," he replies, pointing to where I see the blood.

"Anywhere else?"

I know this seems like a silly question, but it's not uncommon for the person that has been shot to not actually know how many times they have been hit. In the excitement it's easy to lose count.

That's why paramedics are taught to remove all of the clothing of a shooting victim. Bullet holes close up to a great extent and are sometimes hard to see. Contrary to popular belief entrance wounds bleed very little if at all. Exit wounds are easier to see if there is one. A small caliber bullet doesn't always exit but can do a lot of damage internally. The bullet can take many different paths as it goes through and bounces off your bones and internal organs.

The patient's shirt is unbuttoned so it's easy to check for exit wounds above the waist at least. There aren't any that I can see.

"I don't think so," was his answer.

I turn to Debbie and tell her to go get the stretcher. I want to get him into the ambulance so I can do a proper exam.

While she goes for the stretcher, I get the stethoscope out of the kit and listen to his breath sounds to see if the bullet has punctured his lung. If the bullet has entered the chest cavity you can usually hear air escaping from the bullet hole. In addition the patient will be short of breath. In his case he didn't appear to be having any difficulty breathing. I couldn't hear air escaping and his lung sounds are clear with good air movement. It didn't look like the bullet had entered the chest cavity or punctured his lung. This is something you have to reassess frequently on a patient because the symptoms can be delayed.

Debbie comes back with the stretcher and we help him to pivot onto it. As we are wheeling him to the ambulance officer Mike comes over and starts to question the patient as to what happened.

The patient, still fairly worked up, starts to tell his story, "I was in the bar minding my own business when that son of a bitch comes in and ask me to come outside. Just as we got out the door he pulled a pistol, one that I gave him years ago, and started shooting at me. I grabbed him up and started hitting him. I guess he got me in the back when I turned around. Can you imagine that? Shooting someone with the gun you gave him."

We are at the ambulance and I interrupt the story long enough for Debbie and me to lift him in. I now realize why the other guy looked like he did. Our patient, while being shot, had managed to get some good punches in on the other guy before realizing he had come to a gun fight unarmed and was getting the worst end of the deal. Being only a block from the police station they arrived in time to catch the shooter before he drove off.

The patient now loaded and the doors shut, I grab the scissors to start removing clothing. As Debbie is taking vitals I notice the patients little finger on his right hand is hanging on by a slim thread of skin just below the first knuckle. The patient just now starting to calm down hasn't even noticed it yet. He is still talking about what happened when I call it to his attention.

"How did that happen?' He asks.

"Looks like it was just about shot off," I tell him.

Debbie is finished with vitals and tells me they are stable. I now notice some blood in the patient's groin area. I tell him what I am going to do and start cutting off his pants. When I get them cut off I spot two more wounds to his inner thighs. The entrance wound on his right thigh was about 3 inches from the top of his thigh with the exit wound straight out the back of his leg. The entrance wound on his left thigh was about 4 inches from the top of the leg with the exit wound about 5 inches to the inside of the entrance. Neither one was bleeding that badly. This meant that the bullets had missed the large artery and veins in that part of the leg.

I now see a spot of blood on his underwear and proceed to cut them off. To my surprise I find yet another entrance wound just above the pubic hair line. It is becoming evident, to me at least, what the other guy was aiming at. I look but can't find an exit wound. Since the bullet that made this wound could easily have hit many different organs I am now growing concerned.

The patient had been completely unaware of any of these wounds until I found them. He then makes the connection of what the other guy was trying to hit and gets worked up again.

"Damn S.O.B. tryin to shoot my balls off, I guess."

During the exam the patient kept right on talking. We find out the patient and the man who shot him had, at one time, been good friends. He had given him the pistol as a birthday gift.

"I know what his problem is he's pissed because I'm dating his x-wife. Hell, they been divorced for 10 years. You'd think he'd a got over her by now."

A thought comes to me after I hear this. *And now we know the rest of the story.*

We now have a patient that has been shot at least 4 times with a .380 automatic, lucky for the patient it's not a very powerful round.

Debbie puts the patient on oxygen and sets up an IV while I quickly bandage the wounds. I get the IV and start to reassess the patient. Lung sounds are still present and his vitals are still holding. He's not showing any signs of shock and is still talking a mile a minute.

His condition is unchanged upon arrival at the ER. I am filling out the report when the doctor on duty that night comes out of the exam room.

"It's pretty obvious what he was aiming at isn't it?" he says grinning.

"Yea doc, guess it's a good lesson in why not to mess around with your friends x-wife and if you do, don't give him a gun for his birthday," I joke back.

I found out before I left the ER that the bullet that entered at the pubic hair line exited between his legs just behind the scrotum, missing all vital organs. I felt bad that I had missed that exit wound until the doctor told me it took him over 15 minutes to find it. The bullet in his back hit a rib and traveled around under the skin and stopped under his armpit. It never entered his chest cavity. He was lucky.

A Woman Scorned

When I worked for Montgomery County EMS in the early 80s the most interesting place to be stationed was in the East County sub-station. East Montgomery County was a very rural area of the county. People there were not prone to calling the ambulance unless they really needed one. Even though it was not normally a busy station, when you did get a call it was usually interesting.

It's Saturday morning and I am riding an extra shift at the East County station. I am riding with a young paramedic named Ronnie. He's not my usual partner. I am just filling in for the day while his regular partner is on vacation.

It's another typical summer day in southeast Texas. I arrive at the station, a converted trailer, just before shift change at 8:00 a.m. and it's already over 80 degrees. Next door to our station is a sub-station for the sheriff's department also a converted trailer home. Why look out of place since most of the people in that part of the county live in trailers anyway.

Ronnie and I have checked out the ambulance, a ritual done at the start of every shift and gone inside to cool off. We have been sitting down for a few minutes when the pager comes to life.

"Medic 4 shooting at the Exxon station in Porter," the dispatcher tells us.

"Just wouldn't be a good Saturday morning without someone getting shot would it?" I ask rhetorically.

As we head out the door, we see a deputy running toward his patrol car.

"Going to the shooting at the gas station?" Ronnie asks him.

"Yea, is that where you all are going?" the deputy asks.

Ronnie shakes his head yes and tells the deputy to lead the way.

The deputy leaves out of the parking lot slinging gravel everywhere. Ronnie follows at a safe distance. The gas station we have been dispatched to is about 8 miles away. The deputy arrives at the scene about a minute before we do. He quickly radios telling us the victim has left the scene so we can slow down. By the time he tells us this we have the station in site so it really doesn't make any difference.

We always appreciate first responders and law officers letting us know what we were coming into on a call. If no one is hurt it is nice to know we can slow down. On the other side of the equation is when you have patients that are badly hurt or the officer perceives them to be so, then you get the radio call to "step it up". When responding to an emergency we travel as fast as conditions will allow. Telling us to "step it up" is unnecessary. We will get there as fast as we safely can.

We pull into the parking lot and see several people trying to tell the officer what happened. I still have no idea who was shot or what happened to him. I take a quick look around the gas station and don't see anyone in distress. The witnesses seem to be more worried about telling their story to the cops than telling us what happened to the patient.

Ronnie and I approach the group and finally get their attention.

"Who got shot?" I ask.

Four people answer at once telling us that one of the men that works at the station was shot at by his wife. We learn she had driven up while her husband was pumping gas jumped out of her car and started shooting at him. This was all great to know but they still haven't told us where he went.

"Where is he?" I ask in a firm voice. It's like trying to get information out of a 4 year old.

Finally one old redneck with half of his teeth missing spoke up above the rest.

"When she jumped out a the car with the gun, Jimmy know'd he was in trouble and commenced to runnin' that way," he then pointed down the road.

I look in the direction he's pointing and see a junk yard and a large metal building that looks like it's a garage of some sort. It's about a block away. As I scan the road and junk yard in an attempt to spot the victim, I notice someone at the metal building waving and motioning for us.

I call this to the attention of the officer and tell him we'll check it out. As we arrive at the garage, the young man that has been waving frantically points inside.

"He's bleedn' real bad." he tells us.

"This must be the place," I say to myself.

I enter a small grimy office and see a man in dirty blue coveralls leaning back in an old leather office chair. The next things I see are two large puddles of blood on the concrete floor at his feet. The man is breathing hard and is wringing wet with sweat. This is due, for the most part, by his sprint from the gas station in an attempt to avoid getting shot. He's still conscious so I identify myself and ask him where he's hit. He complains of pain in his upper thighs.

Since we have active bleeding, the first objective is to control it. Ronnie and I both grab our "paramedic scissors" and start cutting off the patients coveralls starting at the bottom of the legs. I get to about the knee area when the patient starts telling us to stop.

"What's wrong?" I ask him.

"I ain't got no underwear on," he tells us.

Ronnie and I exchange glances and keep on cutting. I have to hold back a grin. Here is a man that has been shot, is bleeding profusely and is worried about not having any underwear on. A thought his me. *Maybe he should have taken the advice Mother's give their children about wearing clean underwear in case you are in an accident and need to go to the hospital.*

Once the wounds are exposed we find he has been hit two times, once in each thigh. The entrance wounds are in the back of each thigh about 3 inches below his buttocks. The exit wounds are about an inch in diameter. They are the ones that are bleeding. Not spurting arterial bleeding but a good steady stream of venous blood. The bullets appear to have missed the thigh bones and femoral artery even though they have passed pretty much through the middle of his thigh.

To stop the bleeding we wrap each leg tightly in 4x4s and Kerlix. Four by fours are not lumber but a 4 inch square gauze pad used to place over a wound. They also come in 2 inch and 3 inch square pads but the 4 inch ones are the most popular. Kerlix is the brand name for the bandage used to wrap around the wound to hold the 4x4s in place. It is also made of gauze several yards long and about 4 inches wide. Now that the bleeding is stopped I have time to make sure he didn't get hit anywhere else.

After a head to toe exam I cannot find any other wounds. Now that he has started to calm down I am curious to hear his side of the story so I asked him what happened.

"Me and the wife had a real bad fight this mornin', I went on to work and she showed up with a gun and started shootin' at me. I took off runnin' but she got me anyway. I didn't know where else to go so I ran over here."

We transported him to the hospital and he was released in a few days. I found out later from the deputy that his wife had bought the gun that morning especially to shoot her husband with. What is it they say about a woman scorned?

Another Woman With A Gun

Since I am on the subject of women shooting their husbands, I will tell you about another one. It is midafternoon, the hottest part of the day in southeast Texas. The time of day when it feels like the humidity and the temperature are in the high 90s. Just walking outside makes you sweat. It's on such a day that Karla and I are told to respond to a shooting in an old residential area of Conroe. The police are already on the scene telling us to "step it up."

Sharla, who is driving, makes a big act out of pretending to be whipping the horses on a wagon to make them run faster. We are both still laughing as we pull up to the scene. As I get out I start to concentrate on the patient and immediately get serious. I see a man lying on the porch of a small wood frame house. He's holding his lower abdomen and appears to be in a considerable amount of pain. The two police officers standing at a safe distance in the middle of the yard appear to be ignoring the patient. Their concern is obvious; they had told us to "step it up" hadn't they?

As I approach the patient I start looking for obvious wounds and bleeding but don't see any. I kneel down by him and try to get his attention. It is funny how some patients refuse to cooperate even when someone is trying to help them. I see right away that this man is going to be one of the uncooperative ones.

"I'm Patrick. I'm with the ambulance. Can you tell me what happened?"

"Whada you think happened the bitch done shot me," he screams.

He's holding his abdomen and I can pretty much bet he's been hit at least once in that area. Like I have said, with gunshot wounds you have to do a close exam to find them all.

"What's your name?" I ask, trying to get his attention again.

"What f--- do you need my name for? Just move your ass and get me to the hospital," he tells me. At that moment I see why the officers were ignoring him.

I have an escalating system when it comes to dealing with a patient. I always start out nice. Most people respond to this and even if they are in pain realize I am there to help and usually do their best to cooperate. Some do not and in these cases I have to escalate my demeanor to match that of the patients. One of the things you cannot do is to let a patient or bystanders dictate how you will or will not treat them. In this case I had to take it to the next level.

"Ok, listen to me," I say in a more forceful voice. "I am with the ambulance. I need you to stop rolling around and let us check you out. Then we will take you to the hospital." Then raising my voice a little more to make my point, I say, "Do you understand me?" most of the time this works to get the patients attention.

"All I know is that I was sitting on the porch mindin' my own business and the bitch drove by and shot me. Now get my ass to the hospital."

It's clear that I am not getting through to him. He is still rolling around so much that Sharla and I can't even begin to find out where he was shot. It's clear that we are going to have to physically grab him. I don't like doing this to patients but sometimes it is the only way to get them to cooperate.

Sharla and I both grab an arm to stop him from rolling around while I make eye contact with him. Putting my face directly in front of his so there is no mistake as to who I am talking to I let him know who is in charge. "Now listen to me. You are going to lay still and you are going to let us treat you. You are not going to tell us what to do. We are going to tell you what to do. Do you understand me?" I yelled the last question to let him know I was serious. He did not answer right away so I asked him again. "Do you understand me?" he slowly shakes his head yes and I can feel his arms start to relax.

"Now tell me where you got shot and how it happened?" I ask, now back to my bright and cheery self.

"My ex-wife did it man she shot me in the belly. Just make it stop hurting," he exclaims.

"Ok, let us see where you got hit," he moves his hands from in front of his lower abdomen and I can see a small hole in his pants just below the waistline. "I'm going to unbutton your pants so I can see better," I tell him. He nods his head.

I find the entrance wound; it's about 2 inches below his belly button. Like most entrance wounds it has all but closed up and looks more like cigarette burn than a bullet hole. I tell Sharla to go get the stretcher. The patient is only wearing cut offs and a tee shirt so it's fairly easy to make a full exam. I don't see an exit wound or any other wounds for that matter. The one wound he does have is potentially serious. Sharla returns with the stretcher. We lift him on to it and head for the ambulance.

The patient is now becoming very quiet. He is still conscious but is starting to get the "far away" look in his eyes, one of the signs of shock. I am not surprised since a wound to that area can hit the intestines the bladder and the descending aortic artery.

Sharla takes vitals quickly and I am not surprised to see his blood pressure is low and heart rate is rapid, more signs of hemorrhagic shock. I decide to apply what are called military anti shock trousers. Abbreviated M.A.S.T. They are placed over a patient's legs and abdomen. Air is pumped into the three bladders built into each leg and stomach. The purpose is to force blood that is in the patient's legs and abdomen into the upper part of the body to be utilized by the brain and heart, two organs that die quickly without proper blood supply.

The MAST pants use Velcro to hold them around the patient's legs and stomach. Then a small foot pump is hooked up via a rubber hose and air is pumped into the bladders to a specified pressure, this forces blood to the upper part of the body.

It only takes us a couple of minutes to put them on and inflate them. This brings the patient's systolic blood pressure back up over 100. I quickly start an IV and we are heading for the hospital. I am now ringing wet with sweat and look as if I have been hosed down, typical for this time of year.

I radio the ER and tell them we are coming in. As a result they catch a thoracic surgeon that was walking out the door and ask him to wait and asses the patient. They also have one of the surgery teams hold over. Except in big urban hospitals with level 1 trauma centers the surgeon and associated personnel go home at about four p.m. If a patient needs surgery after that an on call team is brought in.

We roll the patient into the trauma room at the hospital. The ER doctor and surgeon are waiting as we lift the patient onto the ER gurney. The surgeon has never seen M.A.S.T pants before and starts questioning me as to how and why they are used and how to remove them. There is a proper procedure for removing the pants. It is time consuming with air being let out of the each section very slowly and constant checks of the patient's blood pressure. Doing the deflation process as directed can take 30 minutes or more. I stared to explain to the doctor how we are taught to deflate them but he cuts me off.

"All I want to know is how to take the g-- d---- things off," he shouts. My offer to go to the operating room to assist falls of deaf ears. "Just tell me how to take them off and quit wasting my time," he says.

I see that he isn't going to listen so I tell him what he wants to know.

"Turn these three valves 90 degrees, the air will come out and then just undo the Velcro and pull them off. Just don't cut them."

I understand the surgeon wanting to just get the pants off so they can start operating. It always seemed time consuming the way we were taught to do it. I do know most surgeons just take them off and start cutting. M.A.S.T pants have been controversial for years and various studies have shown they do not increase a patient's chance of survival. This is the only time I ever used them.

For the Love of Money

Just after sundown Chuck and I have finished supper and just turned on the TV. The pager comes to life and the dead pan voice of the dispatcher tells us to respond to a multiple shooting. The address is only blocks from the station. Chuck and I look at each other. How could there be a shooting, its Tuesday night nothing ever happens on Tuesday night. We head out the door of the station into the cool spring night. People are out walking their dogs in the park across the street from the ambulance station. It is so peaceful and quiet it's hard to believe that only a few blocks away three people had been shot.

"Medic 7 to dispatch we are clear on the call. Has a deputy been dispatched to the scene?" I ask.

"Medic 7, yes but the nearest one is 15 minutes away. You are advised to stage until he gets there."

Chuck looks at me in disbelief. "Does she realize what she is saying? We can't wait 15 minutes."

"I know we can't."

"Dispatch, are you sure the deputy is 15 minutes away? That's a long time to wait if people are bleeding in there." I was trying to convey a sense of urgency to the dispatcher since she didn't seem to be the least bit worried about letting people possibly die while we waited for law enforcement.

"Medic 7, the sheriff's dispatcher is still telling me he is 15 minutes away. You are still advised to wait." She puts an emphasis on the "wait" like we didn't hear it the first time.

"Ask her who called for the ambulance," Chuck says.

I realize what he is thinking. If the call originated from the person who was shot, chances are the person who did the shooting is gone. Even if a neighbor called, chances are the scene is clear.

"Dispatch, who called for the ambulance?"

"Medic 7, one of the people who were shot made the call. She said two others were also shot."

Now that we have finally been given information, Chuck and I decide to pass by the house once with lights and siren going just in case the bad guys are still hanging around.

As we pass by nothing seems wrong, neighbors visiting, kids playing, a typical suburban scene. Chuck circles the block, and then we stop in front of the house and radio the dispatcher that we are on the scene and entering the house.

You can hear the tone in her voice as she advises us for a third time not to enter. Chuck and I know we are taking a calculated risk by going into the house but it is a risk we are willing to take.

Dispatchers like to think they control every move the ambulance makes. While we are all part of the system it is still the paramedic's ultimate responsibility to decide what to do with regard to patient care. It is the dispatcher's job to provide the ambulance crew with as much information as possible. The problem starts when dispatcher thinks they have authority over the crews. In this incident she was technically following normal procedures by telling us to not enter the house. What she was not doing was thinking it through. If people are wounded, waiting 15 minutes can mean the difference between life and death. If one of the people who got shot was able to use the phone, chances are the person that shot her is gone. It is a risk to go in but we are reasonably sure it's safe.

As I approach the house, I think to myself how quiet it is. Knowing that people had been shot I guess I expected to hear or see something unusual. I quickly walk to the garage door, Chuck is right behind me. I hug the front wall until I reach the front door.

Standing beside the door protected by brick I pound on it several times and jump back and wait several seconds for some sort of response. When bullets don't come flying through the door, I look at Chuck and ask him if he is ready to go. He nods his head yes. I grab the door knob and to my surprise it turns. We were prepared to kick the door in but following the old firefighter rule of trying the door to see if it is locked before you knock it down paid off.

My heart starts to race as I throw the door open. I wait a moment to see if anything happens, again nothing. I listen but the only sound I can hear is the television. Not loud like you might expect in an effort to cover up the sounds of gun shots but at a normal volume. Because it is so quiet I start to think that it's either a prank call or we might have the wrong house. Knowing we still need to be careful I remain behind the protection of the brick wall and yell into the house asking if anyone is home. I am almost surprised when I hear a faint cry for help that sounds like it is coming from the back of the house.

I look at Chuck. "You ready?" I ask.

"Yep, let's go," he says.

I make a right turn; enter house and almost trip over the body of a man lying in the hallway. The hallway is about 8 feet long. He's lying face down against the wall with his head toward the front door. I see streaks of blood running down the wall. The next thing I notice is the man's belt pulled half way out of the loops on his pants. I kneel beside the body as Chuck goes past me to find the person that is still calling for help. I grab the patient's shoulder and roll him towards me. His face is such a mess it takes me a moment to figure out what happened to him. He has an entrance wound in the middle of his forehead and both of his eyes are blown out of their sockets. Brains and blood are coming out of his nose, mouth, ears, and eye sockets. I feel for a pulse knowing I won't find one. I roll him back against the wall so the deputies will know how I found him.

I get up and head down the hall to find Chuck. The television is still playing as I enter the living room. I stop to look for other victims; from where I am standing I can see into the kitchen and dining room. Except for the dead man lying by the front door, nothing seems amiss. No other bodies, no blood, no signs of a struggle, everything neat as a pin. Again it strikes me as to how quiet it is.

I hear Chuck and look to the left down another hall leading to the bedrooms and see him tending to a woman who is sitting on the floor. She is conscious and Chuck is trying to assess how many times she's been shot. As I kneel down to help Chuck, the woman spots me and starts asking me to find her daughter.

"Please find my daughter. I told her to run and hide. Please find her," she pleads.

"Ok I'll look for her," I tell her.

I have already looked in every room except the bedrooms and bathroom and had not found anyone. I start the search in the bedroom I am standing closest to. I go in and find a desk, chair, and phone but not much else. I look under the desk and in the closet but don't find anyone. Back out and down the hall to the next room. Toys and stuffed animals are lying all over the floor, a typical child's room. I look under the bed and in the closet, the usual places for a kid to hide, but don't find her. I am starting to hope that she may have gotten away and is just too scared to come out. I come out and head for the only room I haven't looked in yet, the master bedroom.

At first glance it is like the other rooms I have searched, no signs of a struggle. I notice there is a light on; in fact there has been a light on in every room I have been in so far. As I scan the room I see on my left a king size bed with a bright red comforter. I look across to the far side of the bed and see what I had hoped I wouldn't. A small child is laying on her right side in the fetal position with her back to me. As I head around the foot of the bed to check her I am still hoping she is just too scared to move. My hopes are quickly dashed as I get close to her and see a large puddle of coagulated blood on the bed. I kneel down to check her and immediately see a bullet wound in the middle of her forehead. It didn't cause the collateral damage that it did to her father but a fatal wound none the less. I then notice blood is all over the front of her shirt. I can see that she has also been shot in the chest. I know she is beyond help but feel for a pulse anyway. As I do this I see another bullet wound in the middle of her forearm.

90

Then it hits me like a ton of bricks; the wound in her arm and chest are probably caused by the same bullet. It becomes clear to me that she was covering her face, cowering in fear when she was shot.

It is one of the few times in my career as a paramedic that my emotions get the best of me for a moment while on a call. I stand up as tears start to well up in my eyes. The thought of who could shoot a child as she cowered in fear was almost overwhelming. I pull myself together by concentrating on the one patient that is still alive and the hope that we can save her.

I leave the room and find Chuck still attending to the mother. As I kneel down Chuck looks up at me with the question in his eyes. I know he wants to know if I have found the daughter and if she is dead. I look at him and shake my head from side to side. He then knows she is dead.

In situations such as this a paramedic tries his or her best to not tell the survivors that their family members or friends are dead. It doesn't matter if it is a car wreck or a house fire or a shooting you try your best not to tell them the condition of the others. You side step the question when they ask how someone is. You tell them, they are being looked after, or we are doing everything we can for them." They are not lies but not really the truth either. These answers seem to satisfy most people in this kind of situation. The reason for this is so they can be told about their loss in a much more controlled setting.

Chuck quickly shows and tells me about the wounds he has found. She has one wound to the back of her head just behind her right ear. I found out later the bullet had hit at an angle and because the bone is thick at that point it didn't penetrate. She has an entrance wound to her right back shoulder and an exit wound just above her collar bone. It appears to be clean wound with minimal bleeding. The third wound is to her right lower back and as far as Chuck and I can see there is no exit wound.

Even though the patient is still conscious and alert I am concerned she may not be for long. I don't know how much damage the wound to the head has caused. I am concerned that she may become unable to tell us what happened and decide to try to get a description of the person or persons that shot her and her family.

"Mam, can you tell me who did this?" I ask her at least hoping to get a description.

"Yes, it was Harry Carter," she says giving me a name.

I am shocked that she gave me a name. I had only expected some sort of description not a name.

"You say a man named Harry Carter shot you. Was there anyone else with him?" I ask probing a little further.

"Yes, he was with a Mexican. I told Amy to run when they started shooting. Did you find her? Is she OK?" she asks.

"Everyone is being taken care of," I tell her.

"Chuck, did you hear what she said?" he shakes his head yes.

I take a small note pad out of my shirt pocket and write down the name Harry Carter. I show it to Chuck to make sure I wrote what he heard. He reads it and agrees it is the name she gave me. We both know that if the patient dies or becomes unable to function we would be the only ones who would know who shot her. I took what is called a dying statement.

I hear voices at the front door. It's two of our first responders that finally got brave enough to come into the house. I meet them at the front door and tell them to get the stretcher. As I turn around to go back to the patient, a man comes running up in civilian cloths and flashes his deputy badge.

He tells me, "I live next door. I just looked out and saw the ambulance and wondered what happened."

I pull him aside and quickly explain what I have seen so far.

"They shot and killed their daughter?" he asks in disbelief.

"Yes they did," I tell him.

"Where is she?"

"In the master bedroom."

He takes off through the house and I follow. It is obvious he knows the house and goes right to the bedroom. Moments later he comes out crying. He approaches me and asks if any other law enforcement is on the scene yet. I tell him no and explain about the extended E.T.A. we were given for a deputy to get to us. He just shakes his head in disbelief.

The first responders return with the stretcher and have to do some maneuvering to get it over the body of the husband lying by the front door. As we are getting the mother on the stretcher when the deputy originally dispatched to the scene finally arrives. He apparently is not prepared for what he sees and for a moment just stands in the hall looking at the dead husband. I have decided there is no way to get the mother out the front door and over or around her dead husband without her seeing him. The mother is starting to get a little confused and I want to transport as soon as possible. I go to the deputy who has just arrived and tell him to make a note of where the husband's body is located because we are going to move it to get the mother out. He says to go ahead. One of the first responders and I throw a rug over his head and drag him around the corner into the dining room. I didn't want to move him, but I felt it was the quickest way to get the patient out of the house.

Just before we head for the unit, I go up to the deputies who are now talking with each other and tell them we are getting ready to take the mother out to the ambulance. I assumed that one of them would want to question her about what happened. One of them did ask what hospital we were taking her to but neither one ask anything else.

The mother is still conscious but confused as we head out the front door. She has quit asking about her daughter. I thought it odd that during all this she never ask about her husband.

A fairly large crowd of neighbors has gathered on the front lawn by this time and a murmur sweeps through them as we exit the house. One person calls the mother by name and tells her she will be praying for her.

Two more sheriff's cars slide to a stop in front of the house as Chuck and I load the patient into the back of the ambulance. They both get out and head for the house. Not one of them has yet to ask the mother, Chuck, or myself any questions. Chuck and I are the only other people besides the patient who know who shot her.

I quickly establish an IV and we head for the hospital. Even though the mother is seriously wounded, she remains conscious during the trip to the ER. We are about halfway to the hospital when a chilling thought hits me. What if the people who shot her and her family had been waiting around the corner to see if anyone survived and are following us to finish the job? There is nothing I can do about it now, but I should have thought about it before leaving the scene. Actually one of the deputies should have thought about it and ridden with us to the hospital. In my effort to get her to the ER quickly the idea didn't enter my mind until later.

We arrive at the ER without incident. Luckily my concern about being followed was unfounded. The ER staff immediately goes to work on the mother. Even though she has remained conscious she is still confused and is now starting to show signs of going into shock. I am worried that the wound to her lower back may have caused serious damage. The ER doctor quickly shares the same concern. He tells the charge nurse to call in the surgery team. In the meantime, x-rays reveal no fractures to the mother's skull. They do reveal the bullet that entered her back is lodged in her lower abdomen. This means the bullet more than likely passed through her liver and intestines, potentially fatal even with surgery.

Upon returning to the station the dispatcher asks us to call her on the telephone. I call and am asked to meet a detective at the sheriff's substation in the southern part of the county. I hang up and tell Chuck.

"Well it looks like somebody finally wants to know what happened and what we saw."

We meet with the detective and tell him what we saw and what the mother told us about who shot her. I tell him there is a fairly good chance she may not live through surgery. Chuck and I are asked to write out statements with emphasis on who she said shot her. We did this and based on these statements Harry Carter was arrested early the next morning at his upper middle class home. The sheriff's department was a little slow in getting started but did make the arrest quickly. The other man involved in the murder was arrested two weeks later while trying to cross the border into Mexico. Harry Carter had apparently told them who his accomplice was.

The mother spent several weeks in the hospital and went through several surgeries but lived to testify against the people who shot her and killed her husband and daughter.

I also testified at the trial. In fact, since I was the first person to enter the house after the shooting and the first one to ask and hear who shot her, I was the first witness called. Both men were tried at the same time in the same court room.

Harry Carter, the person the mother named as one of the people who shot her, was a well-known man in the local area. He was in fact a "friend" of the people he shot and killed. The mother testified that her daughter and Carter's daughter had played together on many occasions. Carter apparently lived two lives. One life was a well-known business man, deacon of the church, president of the little league, and a member of other community organizations. The other was dealing with less than desirable characters in loan sharking and other illegal endeavors. Apparently his reason for the visit that evening was to collect on a debt that the husband owed.

The mother testified that Carter and his accomplice had knocked on the door and asked to talk to her husband Craig. When they found out he was not home they forced themselves inside and demanded she get him to come home. Craig owned a string of sleazy bars in the Houston area. His wife called around found him and claiming she was sick to get him to come home. While they waited, Carter told the mother he would not hurt anyone. Since she knew and trusted him she believed what he said.

Apparently the mother and daughter were forced into the bedroom when Craig drove up. The mother told the court that as soon as she heard the front door open there was a gun shot. A moment later both men burst into the bedroom and started shooting. This is when she told her daughter to run and hide. The mother was obviously running away when she was shot. That is the reason all of her wounds were in the back. I don't think the daughter ever made it out of the room. Even though this happened many years ago I still get somewhat upset when I think of this little girl covering her face in fear while two men towered over her and then shot her to death. It is even worse when you think about the fact that she knew one of them.

Both men testified during the trial and since the only person that lived through the incident couldn't positively say who shot her they pointed the finger at each other. They admitted to going to the house to collect money Craig owed Carter. In fact that is the reason Craig's belt was pulled out of his pant loops. It was rumored he wore a money belt, they were looking for it.

Both men were convicted of killing Craig and sentenced to life. A few days before Carter was due to be transferred to the big house, he successfully hung himself in the county jail. His buddy in crime later pled guilty to the murder of the daughter and received forty additional years. He won't be able to kill another innocent eight year old ever again.

I became much more involved in this call than usual since I testified at the trial. To this day when I think about this call it is still one that bothers me.

Target Practice

"A shooting at the Railroad Street Bar, I can't believe it, a nice quiet respectable place like that and someone gets in with a gun. They'll probably pull their membership card," I slam the door shut as Jason gets the unit started.

"Yea, last fight we had there was over a spilled beer. Wonder what started it this time forgetting to say excuse me after they burped," we both laugh.

The Railroad Street Bar is a drinking establishment right next to the railroad tracks that run through the small town of Navasota. It occupies the bottom floor of an ancient run down office building. In fact, it is just called the Railroad Street Bar. No one seems to know its real name. One of its claims to fame is serving beer to anybody able to walk up to the bar and order it. It is ironic that a bar known for being so violent is only a block from the police station. The good part of this is the cops always beat us to the scene.

Ronny, one of the officers on the scene calls us on the radio. "Medic 7 the scene is secure. You have one patient. He's outside and across the street from the bar."

"Sure would be nice if all the cops would let us know what's going on like he just did," said Jason.

I agree with him. A lot officers use the "need to know" approach that is "you don't need to know." In my opinion they just don't worry or think about it, figuring we will find out when we get there. On the other hand they seem to worry a lot about how long it is taking the ambulance to get to them. It is not uncommon to hear them either ask dispatch to see how much longer it will be for us to get there or ask her to have us "step it up". Even though they all know we have the sheriff's radio frequency on our radio, they rarely radio us directly.

"He could've told us if the patient was dead or not but hey just getting them to radio us is an improvement. We wouldn't want to go into a scene knowing everything. That would take the excitement out of it."

"Yea," Jason agrees, "Wouldn't want us knowing everything, our heads might explode."

We round the corner onto Railroad Street two blocks away from the scene. Three patrol cars with light bars flashing mark the spot. As we stop and get out of the unit, Robert yells at us.

"Don't step on the shell casings they're evidence."

I look around and see at least 10 brass casings with chalk circles around them lying in and around the front door of the bar. The patient is lying under a street light on the opposite corner just across the street. A couple of his buddies are trying to get him to lay still.

"Come on man, quit tryin' to get up. The meat wagon's here. They'll help you."

"What happened?" I asked the young black man as I kneel down beside him. The smell of stale beer from the patient and his two buddies is almost overpowering.

"What the hell you think happened, that S.O.B. shot me. Claims I was makin' eyes at his woman. Don't know who'd make eyes at that ugly hoe."

"Well at least he still has his sense of humor," whispers Jason. He then asks the patient where he was hit.

"I think he got me in da leg. Ma knees hurtin' like a m------ f------."

"Ok, man we have to see where you got hit. We're going to have to cut some or your clothes off so we can see," Jason explains.

Jason takes one pants leg and I take the other. Grabbing our trauma shears we start cutting off his cloths starting with his pants. We both follow the usual procedure of starting at the cuff and going up to the groin area. He's wearing a pull over shirt so unbuttoning isn't an option. Jason cuts up the front of it then branches off to each sleeve kind of like a giant Y. As I have said before you have to remove a shooting victim's cloths when possible. They are often hit several times and don't immediately realize it.

"Hey man, who's goin' to pay for these cloths ya'all just ruined?" asks the patient indignantly.

The irony of this strikes me as funny. Here is a man who's been shot. No one, including the patient, knows if the wounds are serious or not and all he's worried about is a pair of faded blue jeans and a thread bare T shirt.

"How 'bout getting the guy who shot you to pay for them." I tell him.

"Yea, that's a good idea. Get that S.O.B. to pay for um."

Jason and I exchange glances; it's all we can do not to laugh.

During this conversation, Jason and I complete our initial exam. The only wound we can find is just above his left knee. There is no exit wound which means the bullet could be anywhere.

"What caliber of gun was it?" I asked the nearest officer.

"Looks like it was a .380 automatic," he tells us.

A .380 is not a particularly powerful bullet; chances are it didn't travel far. Jason takes vitals while I check again for other bullet wounds. The patient continues to gripe and complain about his ruined cloths. I complete the second survey and again do not find evidence of other gunshot wounds.

One of the reasons for me to check and recheck the patient for other bullet wounds is the fact that the shooter was only 20 feet or so from his victim. He fired ten shots at a stationary target and only managed to hit him once.

As usual when dealing with a drunk he didn't know or care how lucky he was. I decide to tell him.

"Well it looks like he only got you one time in the knee. Do you know how lucky you are?" I asked him.

"What you mean man, lucky. You dun cut my cloths to pieces to tell me that. You gonna buy me some new cloths?"

"I've already told you, I don't work at Wal-Mart. I'm trying to get you to understand that since you were shot at from just across the street you're lucky you were only hit once. Besides your pants were ruined, they had a bullet hole in them anyway."

Everyone in the immediate area even the patient and his buddies start laughing.

Chapter 4….How did that Happen?

Sometimes a paramedic makes a call and after hearing what happened to the patient you wonder how anyone could do something that dumb. Don't get me wrong we all do dumb things; it's what keeps ambulances, fire departments, and hospitals in business. Here are a few stories that will help me make my point.

He had a Plan

It's the day after Christmas a beautiful clear day, not a cloud in the sky. Bob, the proud owner of a new chain saw that Santa brought, decides to try it out. Bob lives in the country on about 2 acres of land, which means he has plenty of oak trees to keep trimmed. He fires up the saw and spots the limb he wants to cut. He raises the saw high above his head but can't quite reach the limb. No problem, he thinks to himself, and backs his pickup up to the tree so he can stand in the bed and reach it. He still has to stretch in order to reach it and ends up standing directly under the limb as he cuts. The limb about 5 inches in diameter and 3 feet long is quickly severed from the tree. As it falls it hits poor ole Bob right in the middle of his forehead. He is knocked out and the still running chainsaw just misses him and falls on to the roof of the pickup. It makes a large dent in the roof and luckily quits running.

Bob's wife who has been watching from the house runs out to find him unconscious and bleeding from his forehead. She quickly calls 911.

Ken and I arrive on the scene and find the patient lying right where he fell. He is starting to wake up and his wife is attempting to keep him from moving. Seeing the pickup under the tree, the chainsaw on the roof, the freshly cut tree limb, and the patient bleeding from a head wound I get a pretty good idea of what probably happened.

As we climb into the back of the truck I automatically start my head to toe assessment looking for obvious injuries. I get no further than his forehead and come to a dead stop. Sticking out of his forehead about two inches is a piece of wood. It appears to be a part of the tree limb that hit him in the head. It is approximately one inch in diameter with a fair amount of blood oozing out from around it. I immediately become concerned that this man possibly has a tree limb stuck in his brain.

Not knowing what has happened the patient is trying to get up. Since a large limb has hit him on the head hard enough to render him unconscious and impale a stick in his head, there's a good chance he has spinal injuries. I tell Ken to immobilize his neck to prevent any further damage and hopefully prevent paralysis.

Once his neck is secure I continue the assessment but do not find any other injuries. His wife fills me in as to what happened while Ken and I immobilize the patient.

"Yep, he had his new toy out of the box for about 15 minutes before this happened. I was standing at the front door watching while he cut the limb, looked like a scene out of a Three Stooges movie. Guess it was too much trouble to get the ladder out of the garage," she tells us wiping worried tears from her eyes.

The patient is conscious but confused and keeps telling us he's OK. In the next breath he ask us for the fourth or fifth time what happened and for the fourth or fifth time I tell him. It is not uncommon for people with head injuries to do this. They don't remember what happened and continue to ask every few moments. You have to continually tell yourself that the patient honesty doesn't remember. It's like trying to deal with a small child asking "Are we there yet?"

Ken and I quickly finish packaging the patient. I am very concerned about the stick in his head and want to transport as soon as possible. In less than 10 minutes we have loaded the patient and are heading for the hospital. He remains stable during transport but blood is still oozing from his forehead.

I radio the emergency room and advise them of the patient's injuries and condition. When we arrive they are ready for us, even the doctor is waiting to see the "stick in the head". As soon as we get the patient onto the hospitals gurney the doctor takes a very close at the head wound. He looks at me with one of those "how in the heck did this happen" expressions. I quickly relate the story to him. I can see a slight smile start to form as he pictures the patient standing under the limb he is cutting. I don't know about the doctor but the image I had was one of a cartoon. The one where the character is sawing the tree limb off while he sits on the wrong side of it and is surprised when he falls along with the limb.

Quickly the doctor orders a portable x-ray of the patients head. He is greatly concerned about how far the wood has penetrated into the patient's skull and possibly his brain. The patient is becoming more alert but is still unaware of our concern that he might have a serious head injury.

The doctor unable to wait until the x-ray technician brings the films back goes the processor to wait for them to come out. I am sitting at the nurses' station writing my report when he returns and heads for the patient's room. Curious, I follow him and get there just as he pulls the stick out of the patients forehead. I am shocked along with everyone else to see that the stick is only an inch long and had only penetrated the skin about a quarter of an inch. I am relieved but embarrassed, feeling as if I had overreacted.

"Doc, I'm sorry about that but it really looked like it was stuck in his skull," I tell him.

"No problem," he says. "Why do you think I ran down to see the x-ray? I thought it was too."

This brought the "stick in the head" call to a close. The patient lucked out this time, the cut on his head and a slight concussion being his only injury. I always laugh when I think of this call. If his wife had thought to grab the video camera he might have made a couple of bucks on one of those funny video shows. Might have even made enough to cover the hospital bill and have his truck repaired.

Anger Management

It's supper time and as it quite often happens we get a call just as my partner and I sit down to eat. "Trauma call at Carlos restaurant." The dispatcher says in her monotone voice. She goes on to give the address and time of the call.

"Well we'll just no load the sucker, then stay and get some enchiladas," Ken jokes as he tosses his fork on the table. "Wonder what adventure awaits us this time? Remember last time? The waitress fell right in front of the kitchen door. She was laying there complaining about back pain while all the other waitresses and waiters kept stepping over her. It was supper time that day too."

"Yea," I agree. "I could barely get her immobilized. Think they even stepped on my hand a couple of times."

By the time we get to the restaurant, we have learned an employee has her arm stuck in the tortilla press. We have also been told to come in through the restaurant's back door. This is not unusual; in an effort to not upset the customers, most restaurants make this request. First responders from the local fire department are already on the scene and have called for "Jaws of Life" rescue tool. We enter the back door and see the first responders gathered in the far corner. As I approach, I see our patient, a short heavy set woman with her left arm trapped nearly up to the elbow between the two wooden rollers of the tortilla press. The press resembles the rollers on an old fashion wringer washer. A small amount of dough is put in the rollers. A motor turns the rollers and draws the dough through them flattening it until you end up with a flour tortilla.

"What's the deal? Why don't we loosen up everything and get her arm out of there?"

Ricky, the assistant chief of the fire department starts to talk. "We have loosened the only adjustment this piece of crap has. That top wheel that adjusts the rollers to make the tortillas thinner or thicker. This thing is so old it doesn't have a quick release or anyway of reversing the motor. Oh, also it's not bolted together it's welded. As soon as we get the Jaws here we're going to just cut one of the posts. We can't think of anything else to do."

At this point the manager of the restaurant steps in front of Ricky. He is so upset he is almost yelling. "I have already told you, you can't destroy it. It's the only one we have."

"And I have already told you unless there is a secret release button or something you haven't told us about, cutting this post is the only way to get her arm out." Ricky had raised his voice somewhat to make his point but the manager seems to barely hear him.

"There has to be another way. You cannot destroy my tortilla press."

During this little altercation the patient is doing her best to keep her composure. I can only imagine how upset she is standing there in pain with her arm stuck in a machine and to hear her boss be more concerned about the machine.

"What's your name?" I ask her.

"Maria," she answers between whimpers.

"Listen Maria; don't pay any attention to him. As soon as the rescue truck gets here it will only take us a couple of minutes to get you out of here. From what I can see it doesn't look like anything's broken. I know it hurts but just hang on and we'll get you out."

"Ok," she replies.

Upon hearing me explain to Maria that we would have her free in a few minutes the manager turns to me. "So, you've figured out a way so you don't tear up the machine?"

I don't know what gave him that idea unless he thought appealing to another person would change things. "No, sir you need to understand there is no other way."

That was all it took to send him into orbit. "You will leave my restaurant immediately all of you!" he shouts pointing at me and the first responders, "I will call someone else."

I always tried to be as professional as possible on a call in spite of people doing and saying outlandish things. Sometimes however you have to get tough to gain control of the situation; this was one of those situations. I muster my most in control voice and start explaining to him the way things are going to go.

"Now you listen to me. We are not leaving and there is no one else to call. You are going to be quiet and quit interfering or I will call the cops to have you removed. This is now a rescue situation which means Ricky and I are in charge of and responsible for the safety and proper treatment of this patient. What that means is that we have the legal right to do what is necessary to free her from this machine and provide medical treatment. And you can't do anything to prevent it. Do you understand this or should I get the cops to explain it?"

This little speech which I only spout off as a last resort varies little. I have used it enough to have it down pretty good. It works 99% of the time when people interfere with EMS, rescue, and fire departments and will not stop.

This man is the one percent that has to push it to the limit. I don't know if it was due to bulling his employees and getting away with it or if he was just your run of the mill insensitive narrow minded jerk of a manager. I guess it really doesn't matter but it always does my heart good to show someone like him that the world doesn't revolve around them.

"I own this restaurant and this machine and I order you out of here," he screams turning as red in the face as anyone I have ever seen. He then dramatically points to the back door.

Employees were scurrying all over the kitchen trying to look busy and avoid the wrath of their boss. Of course none of the rescue personnel moved. While the manager continues to rant and rave, Ricky keys his handy talkie and request law enforcement.

Seconds later the rescue truck pulls up to the back door. Ricky has already instructed them to bring in the "cutters" a "Jaws" tool that looks like a giant pair of scissors. They can cut through several inches of metal in a few seconds.

As the crew of the rescue truck quickly connect the hoses and couplings so as to be able to bring the cutters in the door the manager runs outside and orders them to leave. The rescue crew is prepared for this and continues without comment. The squad car was only a few seconds behind the rescue truck and pulls up just as the manager is trying to block the back door. The officer on duty didn't fully understand what was going on but did see someone interfering with the rescuers. The manager under the mistaken idea the cop was going to be on his side turns and starts screaming orders at him. Not a good thing to do to a police officer.

"Where have you been? You will make these people leave, they want to destroy my restaurant."

The officer tries the nice but firm approach just like Ricky and I had.

"Sir, you need to step out of the way and let them do their job," true to form so far this evening he doesn't seem to get it.

"I will not step out of the way and you will arrest these men," the manager screams at the officer continuing his rant.

Ricky and I exchange glances knowing what is probably going to happen next.

"For the last time get out of the way," the officer says in a loud but controlled voice moving closer to the manager.

The manager standing defiant at the door raises his hand and points it at the officer. "You will leave and you will take them with you or I will…."

He didn't finish the sentence. The officer at least a foot taller than the manager reaches out and grabs him by the wrist and as if to drag a wayward child back home and yanks him out of the way and up against the door of his patrol car. I guess at this point the manager finally gets it through his thick head he isn't going to stop us and more or less shuts up.

"I have dealt with some idiots in my life but he's the poster child for it. I swear about the time I think I've seen it all I see something else," I say to no one in particular.

In just a couple of minutes the cutters have sliced through the frame of the tortilla press and Maria's arm is free. I cannot find any obvious fractures and only a few bruises.

"I don't see anything too bad but I think you need to go to the hospital so they can x-ray your arm to make sure it's ok," I tell Maria.

"No, it'll be ok. I need to stay and work."

As we leave the scene the manager is screaming he will sue us for various things and is standing over the tortilla press looking as if we shot his dog. The cooks were still cooking and the servers were still serving. They had hardly missed a beat during all of this. We always wondered what he made Maria use as a press the rest of the night, probably a couple of rocks.

Snake Charmer

It's midmorning in the middle of the week in the middle of summer. Shirley, who is fairly new to EMS at the time, is my partner. We are paged and told to respond to a "snake bite". The address we are given is only two blocks away. From experience I know that only a few of the people who claim they are bitten by snakes actually are. I also know that even fewer than that are actually injected with venom.

In the short trip to the victim's home I go over in my head the current treatment for a venomous snake bite. Gone are the days when boy scouts were told to cut an X over the bite and suck the poison out. You can't get enough out to make any difference. Gone is the use of restricting bands to slow down the spread of venom. Good meaning people caused more damage by applying tourniquets and stopping the flow of blood altogether. After that, the preferred treatment was to apply ice to the bite. This was also supposed to slow the spread of venom. Ambulances arrived to find patients with their whole arms and legs immersed in ice water. In some cases this caused tissue damage above and beyond what the venom would have caused. Now we just treat symptoms and transport.

I knock on the front door. A few seconds later a boy about 12 years old opens it a few inches and peers out.

"Did you call for an ambulance?" I ask.

He shakes his head yes and opens the door to let us in. He is holding his left arm up and attached to his thumb where it connects to the hand is a 3 foot rat snake. We were told it was a snake bite. We were not told that the snake was still biting.

"How in the world did that happen?" I ask as we step into the house.

The boy, trying his best to not cry, tells us he was attempting to feed the snake when it grabbed his thumb and wouldn't let go.

"I called my mom and she told me to call for the ambulance. He's my pet I've had him for 5 years," the boy explains.

As I looked closer I could see that the snake had gone as far up the boys thumbs as he could go. The problem was that it was still chewing not knowing it could never get any further.

"We'll get him off," I say to the boy automatically, not having any idea as to how I would do it. While Shirley keeps a safe distance, I come up with an idea. "Why don't we just pry open his jaws with a butter knife."

Everyone agrees that this sounded like a plan. We go into the kitchen and quickly find a butter knife. "Ok, let's lay the snake up here on the counter." The boy grabs the snake in the middle with his free hand and places it on the counter by the kitchen sink. The boy grimaces and I see the snake start to chew even harder on his thumb. It seems that moving the snake upsets it.

"Please make him let go, it hurts!" the boy pleads.

"I'm trying. Now hold on I'm going to see if I can get this knife under his teeth."

I take the end of the knife and while I hold the snake just behind its head try to force it under the snake's teeth. The second I touch the snake with the blade he clamps down. I can see its tiny razor sharp teeth digging into the boys thumb. A trickle of blood starts to run onto the counter. The boy screams as tears come to his eyes. He is trying to be brave but the pain is finally starting to get to him. I make two more attempts to force the end of the butter knife under the snake's teeth. Each time he bites harder. Its teeth are now firmly embedded in the boy's thumb making it impossible to get the knife blade under them without cutting his thumb even more that it already is.

"Stop, stop," the boy screams, "It hurts too bad."

"Ok ok. Let's try something else," I tell him as if I actually have another idea.

The only idea I actually have fits in the realm of my grandmother's philosophy on snakes. *The only good snake is a dead snake.*

Since there isn't a snake hot line to call I decide to go with grandma's plan. I know this won't set well with him but I don't know any other way to solve the problem.

"Greg, I think we might have to kill your snake to get him to let go. Unless you have another plan I don't know anything else to do."

"But I've had him for five years. Are you sure we have to kill him?" he asked, as he starting to cry at the thought of losing his pet.

"I'm sorry but I don't think he's going to let go."

The boy nods in agreement. I had spotted a set of knives in a wooden holder on the counter when I first entered the kitchen. I select a 12 inch butcher knife and head outside with Greg and Shirley right behind me. I didn't want to get snake blood all over the house.

"Greg, kneel down here," I say pointing to the driveway.

I kneel down beside him and finally persuade Shirley to hold the lower end of the snake and stretch it out. Not wanting to give any of us too much time to think about it I raise the knife. I take aim at a spot about six inches behind the snakes head and bring the knife down. Snake blood squirts all over my hand and arm. The snakes head now severed from its body finally let's go of Greg's thumb. Shirley quickly lets go of the body as it starts wiggle along with the head all over the driveway.

Greg stands up, at first relieved he is free of the thumb eating snake. He then takes notice of his former pet, now in two pieces, as it flops around. He quickly turns around and runs into the house. We follow and find him standing in the kitchen. He is sobbing as he holds his bleeding thumb over the sink.

"Listen I know its tough losing your pet but we didn't have any choice," Shirley tells him. "Here let us bandage your thumb," Shirley opens the trauma kit and starts to clean and bandage the cuts and puncture wounds on the boys thumb.

I am still holding onto the bloody butcher knife. Not wanting to leave a mess for his parents, I turn on the hot water and find the dish soap. I wash it and put it back into its holder.

Shirley is still talking with Greg as she wraps gauze around his thumb. "Are your parents coming home? You are going to need to let a doctor look at this and possibly get a tetanus shot."

Yea, I called my mom. She should be here in a few minutes."

Shirley is putting things away and closing up the trauma kit, when Greg asks me a question. "Do you think I'll be able to give him a funeral?"

"I don't see why not," I answer.

Then I realize the snake is in the process of squirming all over the front yard as it dies.

"Do you have any grocery bags or something like that?"

Yes, they're under the sink. "

I find a sack. Then as a joke and to see her reaction I hand it to Shirley, "Here go find the snake and put it in the bag so he can bury it later."

I didn't actually expect her to do it, but to my surprise she reluctantly takes the bag and heads outside. Later her version of the story was I was too scared to do it and she had to take charge and handle the big bad snake.

In the days to come Shirley and I related the incident to various fire and EMS people. We were given all kinds of advice on how they would have handled it differently and not killed the snake. The ideas ranged from pouring hot water on it to freezing it with a CO_2 fire extinguisher. One even said I should have heated up the knife blade I attempted to pry its mouth open with.

I finally concluded that no one really knew any more about how they would have handled this call than Shirley and I did. The other conclusion was: Grandma was right.

Chapter 5....Drugs, Alcohol and Other Illegal Substances

I would venture to guess that over half of the patients treated by EMS personnel have illegal drugs, legal drugs, alcohol, or a combination of the three in their system. Even with medical calls once you get to the heart of the matter you find that many of them are the result of substance abuse.

I have treated people of all ages whose major malfunction was too much of something.

The following is a pattern I witnessed several times upon arrival at a house where a "Party" was going on. Before you even get in the front door the smell of marijuana is wafting through the air. Almost always a stereo is blasting rock or rap so loud you can hear it a block away. Several concerned friends practically drag you to the room where Bob or Jane is more often than not lying face down on the floor. Every once in a while they are sprawled out on a couch or bed but not very often. Their friends who are always drunk or stoned on the same thing that Bob took seem to be extremely concerned about the well-being of their unconscious buddy. There is always the hero of the group that makes it a point to tell you they were the one that turned them on their stomach. "I didn't want him to puke and drown in it so I put him on his stomach."

While this is actually a good idea I did see it backfire once.

He Ain't Heavy He's My Brother

We arrive at a "shotgun" house in the slums and, you guessed it, across the railroad tracks. It's Sunday morning about ten o'clock. As we pull up a bone thin old man wearing filthy work pants and a tee shirt with more holes than fabric is sitting on the front porch with a beer in one hand and a cigarette in the other. The call came in as a possible DOA but as usual details   are vague. The old man starts talking before Keith and I get out of the unit.

"Y'all can't help him he's dead, been dead a while." He tells us in a gravelly voice.

"Who's dead?" I ask.

"My brother, he's in the back bedroom stiff as a board."

"We'll go check him just to make sure," Keith tells him as we start up the rickety wooden stairs.

We enter the living room and are greeted by the stench of stale beer, cigarette smoke, vomit, and feces. Being a real shotgun house we had to go through the living room and kitchen before getting to the back bedroom. I see several half gallon liquor bottles sitting around the sink, all of them over half empty. Before we even get to the back room I can see an old steel frame bed against the back wall. A body is laying on it. As we enter the room I see where the vomit smell is coming from. The man is face down in a big fluffy feather pillow. The depression formed by his head and face is full of dried vomit. It covers his mouth and nose. His left arm is hanging down off the edge of the bed. It's dark purple from the blood that has pooled in it. His right arm is lying alongside his body.

I turn to Keith and tell him, "I know I'm just a dumb county paramedic but from here he appears to be dead. You can feel for a pulse if you want to but I'm fairly sure he doesn't have one."

"So just because you've been a paramedic for a 10 years or so you think you know when someone's dead huh?" replies Keith.

I reach down and try to move the patient's arm and to no one's surprise it is just as his brother said it was stiff as a board.

"Yea, I do," Is my reply.

Without disturbing the body we both give it a quick once over to see if there is any signs of foul play.

"Don't see anything unusual, do you?

"Well I guess not. I just have trouble call drowning in your own puke a natural death," Keith says shaking his head.

The smell is quickly getting to the point of unbearable. I am taking shallow breaths through my mouth in an attempt to not smell it. It's not working.

"Let's get out of here," I say as I turn and head to the front of the house. Keith didn't need to be told twice, He was out the door before I was.

The brother is still sitting on the porch exactly as we had left him.

"I told you he was dead, didn't I?" he says as we step out.

"Yes sir. I'm afraid he is. I'm sorry. We are going to have to get the police and judge out here. Do you have any preference on a funeral home?" I ask.

"Ain't nothing to be sorry about. I told him a million times that his drinkin' would kill him. Now it has. He drank a quart of vodka by himself last night. Was so drunk he kept fallin' off the porch. I finally convinced him to go to bed. I found him like that this mornin'."

The old man suddenly stops talking and for the first time seems to be upset at losing his brother. I guess there are worse ways of dying but just to think about it still gives me the willies.

Only the Best

We enter the dilapidated trailer to find a skinny young man wearing holey jeans and a Lead Zeppelins tee shirt lying on a filthy couch. He's moving, always a good sign, and as David and I approach him I smell fresh paint. I scan the room and see a can of Krylon spray paint on the coffee table along with a couple of plastic sandwich bags. One of the bags is coated with gold paint. The patient hearing us approach attempts to sit up. All he can manage is to turn his head to face us. I am surprised at what I see

124

and fight the urge to laugh. He has a gold paint ring around his nose and mouth apparently from where he held the sandwich bag to his face. In addition his hands are covered in the same color paint. It doesn't take a rocket scientist to figure out he's been huffing.

"Am I glad you guys are here man, I felt like I was gonna die there for a few minutes."

I am surprised at how lucid he is.

"What happened?" I ask.

"I was sniffin paint when my chest stared to hurt. I got real scared and called for the ambulance, then I passed out. I woke up just before y'all got here."

"Is your chest still hurting?' asks David as I put an oxygen mask on him.

"Yea, a little," he tells us.

The patient is somewhat short of breath and I hope the oxygen will help with the chest pain.

The propellant in spray paint takes place of the oxygen in the lungs. The "high" they experience is simply due to a lack of oxygen, in some cases the lungs ability to exchange oxygen is seriously impaired. The paint coats the inside of their lungs and block O2 exchange. The chest pain is caused by a lack of oxygen to the heart and sometimes causes a heart attack. In this mas case I hope the extra oxygen will clear up his chest pain.

While David takes vitals I ask the patient something I have always wanted to know, "hey man, how do you decide what color and brand of paint to use?"

"Any color or brand will do the trick but if you really want to fly you use gold or silver Krylon."

I see the patient is going to be alright so I decide to have little fun with him since he is so easy going.

"So, you are telling me it's kind of like buying beer. Bud or Coors will get the job done but once in a while you spring for Heineken."

"Yea, Kinda like that."

I wanted to tell him how ridiculous he looked with a gold ring of paint around his nose and mouth but hey why ruin the feeling. After all he did pay extra for the "good stuff".

I Gotta Get Out of Here

It's Saturday night. Well actually it's early Sunday morning around 2:00 A.M. The bars are closing and we are heading to an auto versus tree in Cut n Shoot, Texas. Sharla and I round the corner and see two Highway Patrol cars parked on the edge of the road with their emergency lights on. Sharla pulls up behind them and stops. What's left of a Buick Century is T boned into a large pine tree. It's about 30 feet off the road and illuminated by the spot lights from the patrol cars.

I get out and grab the trauma bag out of the side compartment. As I approach the car I start looking for patients. The only person I see is as man sitting behind the wheel of the demolished car. The driver's side door is open and the first thing I notice is his left arm dangling by his side. His upper arm is obviously fractured. I get next to him and before saying anything I can smell the whiskey. With his good right arm he is repeatedly turning the ignition key trying to restart the car.

"Hey, what's happening?" I ask.

"I gotta get out of here before the cops get here," he says still turning the key off and on in an attempt to start a motor that will never run again.

"Well I hate to be the bearer of bad news but the cops are already here and your car isn't going anywhere."

"Why the hell not? I just got to get her to start and be on my way."

"Your car is wrecked. You hit a tree and your arm is broken. You're not going anywhere."

He finally stops trying to start the car and looks at me through non focusing eyes, "Just who the hell are you?"

I'm a paramedic with the ambulance and you need to go to the hospital," I tell him.

"Hospital, what the hell do I need to go to the hospital for?" he asks.

All this time the patient had not seemed to notice his left arm was useless and that his car was demolished. Even after leaving him at the emergency room this man never seemed to realize what had happened to him. Thanks to the effects of a quart of Jack Daniels.

These Boots are Made for Walking

Mike and I pull up to the back door of the Navasota city jail, get out and bang on the heavy steel door. Of course it's 2:00 in the morning.

"I swear," says Mike, "There must some un-written law that says prisoners can only request an ambulance after midnight."

"I figure it's about the time they sober up enough to realize they're in jail and think going to the hospital will get them out for a while. Of course it could just be they wanted to bug the EMS crew and assumed we were in bed by now."

The deputy finally opens the door. "What's wrong tonight?" I ask as we walk down the hall leading to the small booking room.

As we get closer to the booking room which leads to the cells I can hear a female voice yelling and screaming.

"You name it. She's complaining about it. Main problem is falling down drunk. Been screaming and carrying on like that since Randy brought her in 2 hours ago."

We get to the small booking room which consists of a waist high counter used to fingerprint the prisoners and fill out paper work. A Polaroid camera sits on a tripod against one wall, on the opposite wall about twelve feet away is a couple of office type chairs. Hanging from the ceiling is the closed circuit camera used to video tape the booking process. The cells are just off of this room. Navasota being a small town has a small jail. There are only two cells each capable of holding four people.

Now that we are closer to the cells I can understand some of the things she is yelling. In between the profanity I hear the typical things like. "Get me out of here. I'm dying. I'm sick. I didn't do anything."

"Can you bring her out here? It gets a little crowded in the cells," I ask the deputy.

From past experience I found out this was better. The cells are so small there is only about a foot clearance between the bunks. It is nearly impossible to stand or examine your patient without hitting your head on the steel bunks. As my Grandpa used to say, "Not enough room to swing a cat."

The deputy grabs the ring of keys off the wall and goes through the open door into the cell block. Yes, it is the stereo typical big iron ring with several big keys on it. I hear the lock turn and in a moment a very pretty, very drunk young woman staggers through the door.

"Sit there," the deputy tells her pointing at the chairs against the wall.

She is wearing what is best described as a riding habit, a long sleeved silk blouse, tight riding pants, and high heel knee length brown leather boots.

She finally sees Mike and I as she sits down.

"Who the hell are you guys?" she slurs.

"We're the paramedics, what's the problem tonight?"

"I need someone to help me get these damn boots off," she yells at no one in particular.

"Do what?" I ask.

I look over at Mike to see if I heard her right. He has this big smile on his face.

"We're the medics; they told us you needed an ambulance. Now, answer me. Do you hurt anywhere?"

"Yea, my f------ feet hurt and I'm too damn drunk to get them off myself. I'm not going to tell you again to take my damn boots off."

She sticks a wobbly leg out straight as if she actually expects me or Mike to help with her boots. She is only able to hold it straight for a few seconds before it falls to the floor and she leans over onto the other chair.

"Are you going to take my boots off for me or not? If not you can get the hell out of here."

It is all Mike can do to keep from laughing. The deputy is just shaking his head and I wonder how in the heck she got the idea into her alcohol soaked brain that we would help her take her boots off.

"Hey, look at me," I tell her. "We're paramedics. We're here because you requested an ambulance. Now, for the last time, do you need medical attention?"

"I told you if you can't take my f------ boots off for me you can go to hell."

After saying this she makes an attempt to sit up and grab her left foot. She almost falls off the chair as she loses her balance trying to hold onto her ankle.

"Sounds like a she needs a maid or a personal servant, she sure doesn't need an ambulance. We're out of here," I tell the deputy.

As we walk out the deputy is trying to get her to stand up so he can take her back to the cell. Being a woman who seems to be used to getting her way, she is even more upset now that I refused to help her.

As she is being escorted back the insults start, "What's the matter, afraid to touch a real woman? You queer or something?"

As Mike and I exit the back door I can hear her still questioning our manhood.

Bad Choice

One of the big effects of alcohol is impaired judgment. The following story is a good example of this.

Kathy, one of our better first responders has arrived on the scene of what is supposed to be a one car accident. A few moments later she radios dispatch and request the fire department rescue squad. She then radios and lets us know we have one patient with his leg trapped in the door of his truck.

Twenty minutes later Jason and I arrive just behind the fire department. We are in the middle of nowhere on a dirt road. The fact that the wreck happened in front of one of the few houses on this remote dirt road is surprising. An old faded blue Chevy pickup is lying on its left side in the front yard. Lying on the ground beside the truck at more or less a right angle is a, drunk, skinny, dirty, foul mouthed young man. His right ankle is trapped inside the left truck door just above where the window starts. From the look of things the truck jumped a deep ditch and ended up on its side. How the driver ended up trapped in this position is a mystery to all of us including the driver.

Kathy is kneeling beside the man attempting to convince him to let her put a c-collar on him.

"Listen b---- I tol' you to let me up," he tells Kathy as he struggles to free his leg.

"And I have told you I'm not holding you down. Your leg is trapped in the door of the truck. You need to wear this brace in case your neck is hurt."

I can hear the frustration in Kathy's voice, something I rarely heard.

"What's going on here?" I ask as Jason and I kneel down beside the patient.

The first thing I notice is the smell. It's a mixture of stale beer, urine, body odor, bad breath, and dirt. Before Kathy has a chance to answer he starts with me, the wrong thing to do.

"I tol' you to let me get the f--- up. I am tired of f------ around with this b----. Just let me up and get the f--- out of here," with this said he starts a new round of struggling.

Kathy is so upset at this man's insults that she stands up hands me the collar and walks away.

"Ok now listen to me," I yell as I grab his flailing arms. "What part of "your leg is trapped" don't you understand? No one is holding you down so quit struggling so we can take care of you. I am going to put this collar around your neck and you are going to lie still so we can get you out," I might as well been talking to the truck. He continues to struggle with me and demanding to be let go.

He's moving so much the c-collar won't do him any good anyway but I want to make a point as to who is in charge. I decide to try to get his attention one more time. Jason takes one arm and I take a hold of the other one. We pin them to the ground as Jason holds his head still and I get Kathy to put the c-collar around his neck. I look him straight in the eye as he struggles to get free and calls all of us just about every derogatory vile name you can think of.

"You can struggle you can cuss but we're in charge and you ARE going to do what we say."

I don't know if he got tired or if what I said finally soaked into his alcohol numbed brain but he quits fighting us for a little while.

By this time the fire department has placed air bags under the truck and is ready to inflate them. As the truck starts to move the patient renews his attempt to get up. The weight is finally lifted off the door and it opens just enough for him to pull his leg out. I would have bet money his lower leg and or ankle was broken but to all of our surprise it isn't, in fact he tries to stand up.

It takes a lot of convincing, wrestling, and a talking by his mother to get him immobilized. Yes, some well-meaning person called his Mom who lived further down the dirt road. Mom shows up as we are trying to wrestle him onto the back board and gives him a talking to as only moms can do. This calms him down long enough to get him into the ambulance. Taking him to the hospital is more of a precaution since he doesn't seem to have any injuries. Although his combativeness is due to drinking and possibly drugs there is a remote possibility it could be from a head injury.

As we try to take vitals a new round of cussing and fighting starts. Marcello, the DPS officer, who arrived on the scene just as his leg was freed, has had enough. He gets into the ambulance and stands over the patient and gives him the ultimatum.

"You can calm down and go to the hospital or you can go to jail."

"Take my ass to jail," he shouts.

Almost before he has finished the sentence Marcello rips the c-collar off his neck and unbuckles the straps that secure him to the backboard. The patient sits up and tries to get off the board. Before he can do this Marcello grabs his arm, puts it behind him and slaps the cuffs on. This seems to surprise the patient.

"What the hell are you doin'? Let me go m----- f-----," he demands apparently forgetting the choice he just made.

"Your ass is going to jail. I'm tired of messing with you," says Marcello, as he half drags the confused man from the back of the ambulance and into the back seat of the patrol car.

Jason looks and me with a straight face and says, "To be honest he was starting to get on my nerves too."

Chapter 6....Jump Starts

Even with all the advancements in cardiac life support in the past twenty years very few people are brought back after their heart stops. The main reason for this, especially in the EMS field, is time. No matter how fancy your cardiac monitor and defibrillator are or how many cardiac drugs you carry, if basic cardio pulmonary resuscitation is not started with in a very few minutes a paramedics chances of resuscitating a full cardiac arrest is almost nil. Even if you do by chance get their heart started they will have severe brain damaged or be brain dead. This is why a true save is very rare.

In spite of all the advertisements and promotion encouraging people to learn CPR most citizens have not taken a CPR course. No matter how fast the ambulance is, there is a time lag. From the moment Grandpa grabs his chest and falls over until the first responders or ambulance are dispatched can be up to 5 minutes, too long to effectively save someone. Even if a bystander or family member sees the patient go out, by the time they figure out what has happened and realize he needs medical help several minutes may have passed. They run to the phone and dial 911, an operator answers and after finding out you want an ambulance pushes a button on her console that rings the dispatcher for the EMS service for your area. There again even with everything working the way it should at least another minute has passed. The ambulance dispatcher confirms your address and phone number then dispatches the appropriate ambulance and hopefully first responder for your area. Depending on what they are doing at the time it might take the ambulance crew another minute or two to get to their unit and head your way. No matter how you add it up and how quick your 911 and EMS system work it adds up to four or five minutes. Experts say that after 4 or 5 minutes without oxygen a patient suffers severe brain damage. The chances of restarting a patient's heart after this length of time are remote.

In recent years EMS dispatchers have attempted to instruct CPR via telephone to family members and bystanders. It's one of those ideas that sounds good on paper. It was determined since most people don't know how to do CPR it might be a good idea to instruct them on how to do it until the ambulance or first responders arrive. On many occasions I was told that CPR was being done on the patient with the dispatcher instructing people over the telephone. I arrived on the scene to find no one doing CPR. On other occasions the person attempting to do CPR was only doing chest compressions or only doing mouth to mouth. Nine times out of ten times if they were actually attempting CPR it was so poorly done as to be ineffective. Every once in a while people would try to imitate the CPR they have seen on TV or in a movie. Sometimes they even made a pretty decent attempt, usually better than people being instructed over the phone.

In all my years as a paramedic I only participated in two calls that resulted in what I call true saves. That is, the patient was in the same shape mentally when they left the hospital as they were before their heart stopped. There were several patients where we got their hearts started again but they never regained consciousness. I don't consider these saves. On both of these calls effective CPR was started immediately, that made the difference.

Hey This Thing Really Works

We enter the front door of the house to find Betty, one of our first responders, doing one person CPR on an elderly woman. The dispatcher had only told us it was a possible heart attack.

"She just arrested right before you got here." Betty tells us in a halting rhythm as she does chest compressions.

Shirley, my partner, immediately gets down on the floor to help with the CPR as I turn on the cardiac monitor. The monitor screen lights up within a few seconds. I pull the paddles from the holders and place them on the patient's chest. Betty has already unbuttoned the patients blouse in anticipation of me needing to use the paddles. One is placed on the upper right chest and the other on the lower left. This gives the current a path through the heart. With monitor/defibrillators you are able to read the patient heart rhythm using the paddles. This is quicker than the electrodes that stick to their chest.

I apply a little pressure to the paddles to make sure I get a good reading and try to hold still. In a moment I see the small irregular squiggly line that tells me she is in ventricular fibrillation. It is the most common arrhythmia found in patients who have just suffered a cardiac arrest. In v-fib there is still some electrical activity causing the heart to quiver but not pump blood.

Asystole is another arrhythmia which is simply no electrical activity in the heart at all. It is very difficult to restart someone's heart in asystole. The third common arrhythmia in a full arrest patient is "pulseless electrical activity." PEA it is just as it sounds, the electrical activity that make the heart beat is present but the patient does not have a pulse. Often PEA will even look like a normal heart rhythm on the monitor; this is why you always check for a pulse. People who have bled to death will often be in PEA. The reason for this is once the heart runs out of blood to pump it will quit beating. If the hearts electrical system is not damaged the electrical impulses will be present for a little while.

I turn the thumb wheel on the paddle to 300 joules and push the charge button. Betty and Shirley see me charging the paddles and instinctively start to clear metal objects away from the patient.

"Everybody clear?" I ask as I look around to make sure no one, including myself is touching the patient.

I also make sure I am not straddling the patients arm. I was on the call where a fellow paramedic learned the hard way to check for this. Mark had cleared the area and was kneeling next to the patient. Because we had never encountered this situation neither of us gave a second thought to the fact Mark was straddling the patients arm. Even though movies and TV exaggerate how much a patient jumps when they are defibrillated it does happen. Some jump more than others depending on muscle tone and how long they have been in full arrest. When Mark pushed the buttons the patient's arm came up and hit him in the groin. Mark rocked back and shook his head but being professional he kept on going. It wasn't until we were returning to the station that Mark said anything about it. "I think I got shocked when I defibrillated that patient. It took me a second to recover."

I realized he didn't know what had actually happened. "Mark, think about it. You were straddling his arm and it jumped up and hit you. You didn't get shocked." I see him think about it for a second a then a smile come over his face.

"He got in that last act of defiance didn't he?"

There is a discharge button on both defibrillator paddles. Both have to be pushed to make it discharge. Contrary to popular belief, they do not have to be pushed at the exact same time. I push and hold the first button and a fraction of a second later I push the second one. The patient's back arches a little and quickly relaxes. I hold the paddles on her chest and wait to see if there is any change in her rhythm. Betty and Shirley also stare at the screen and wait. It takes several seconds for the screen to stabilize and, of course, it always seems much longer when you are waiting. A normal but slightly fast rhythm appears on the scope. Even Betty and Shirley who are EMTs and not really taught to read electrocardiograms see it's a normal rhythm. They both look at me as I reach to feel for a pulse. As I have explained it is possible to have what looks like normal rhythm and for the heart to not be beating. I touch my first and second fingers to her neck and instantly feel a strong pulse.

"She's got a pulse!" I say trying to contain my excitement.

I know that as quickly as a patient regains a pulse they can also lose it. Betty and Shirley are both smiling but also know we are far from having a stable patient.

"Betty, keep ventilating her while I get ready to intubate. Shirley, hard wire her to the monitor and get an IV ready."

Both nod their heads and set to work. I get the intubation kit out of the trauma bag and quickly select the right size endotracheal tube and laryngoscope blade. I walk on my knees the few feet distance from the trauma kit to the patient's head. Betty is ventilating the patient with the BVM attached to a portable oxygen tank.

"Do you want me to start hyperventilating her?" asks Betty anticipating me getting ready to intubate.

I nod my head and she gives the BVM 5 rapid but deep squeezes. This maneuver gives the patient extra oxygen to make up for the 15 or 20 seconds she will do without it while I place the ET tube into the trachea. I lay down on the floor on my stomach and am head to head with the patient. Through trial and error I have found out this works best for me as far as being able to visualize the vocal cords, the key element in successfully placing the ET tube.

With the laryngoscope in my left hand and the ET tube in my right I insert the blade past the patient's teeth. You normally go straight down until the tip of the blade touches the back of the patient's throat. I do this but as I touch the back of her throat the patient gags and takes a deep breath.

"She's breathing!" exclaims Betty.

I can't believe it myself but after the initial deep breath she continues to breathe, they are shallow and labored but they are spontaneous.

"Ok, still assist her since they are shallow," I tell Betty.

During this whole process which took about ten minutes the patient's daughter and son-in-law have remained quiet and given us enough room to do our job. Upon hearing and I am sure seeing that her mother has started to breath asks the question that is always difficult to answer.

"Is she going to be alright?"

We all know she could stop breathing or her heart could stop again at any moment. You don't want to give the family false hope so you deal with the facts. I speak up and give the daughter a typical non-committal answer.

"She doing OK right now but she is still very sick. We're doing everything we can."

I turn and direct my attention to getting an IV started. A very important medication given to post full arrest/V-fib patients is lidocaine. Yes, it is the same thing they give you to numb your teeth at the dentist or kill the pain of getting stitches. It has a similar effect on your heart. It numbs it to a certain degree which makes it less likely to get irritable again and go back into fibrillation.

Shirley has the IV ready. She hands me a tourniquet and I apply it to the patient's upper arm. "What size catheter?" She asks, as I spot a good vein in the bend of her elbow.

"18."

Knowing I usually use an 18 gage catheter Shirley already has one in her hand and hands it to me.

"Betty how's her pulse?" I ask.

Betty puts her fingers on the patient's neck and holds it there for about 10 seconds.

"Still going strong."

The patient's respirations are improving so I tell Betty to put her on an oxygen mask. I look at the monitor; her heart is still running too fast at about 120 beats a minute. I know the lidocaine will slow it down once I give it. I hold the tip of the IV catheter a fraction of an inch above the vein at roughly a 30 to 40 degree angle. In one single quick motion I advance the needle into the vein. I look at the back of the catheter at what is called the flash chamber. When you get into a vein this chamber fills up with a small amount of blood. I see the blood in the flash chamber and lower the catheter to about 10 degrees. I advance the plastic catheter into the vein with my thumb leaving the steel needle in my other hand. The steel needle is thrown away. It is only used to get into the vein and to make the plastic catheter stiff so you can advance it into the vein.

Some blood leaks out of the catheter until I put my thumb over the vein just past the catheter and apply pressure. Shirley hands me the IV tubing and I stick it into the end of the catheter and release the tourniquet.

"Open it up." I tell Shirley and she opens the valve to allow the saline solution to flow into the patient's vein.

I let it run open for a few seconds to make sure I have a good IV and then tell Shirley to slow it down.

"Let's get it taped down."

Shirley picks up a roll of one inch wide cloth tape and tears several pieces about 3 inches long. I put one strip over the connection of the catheter and tubing one over where the catheter goes into the skin. I then loop the tubing and tape it to the patient's forearm. The loop gives you some leeway if it is pulled or stepped on.

There are two types of lidocaine you give to a patient. One is a bolus given to get the drug into the patient's blood stream quickly. The other is a drip to maintain a therapeutic level. I reach for the bolus, it's in a small box that contains a glass vial and a plastic hub with a needle on it. I open the box at the end and empty the hub and vial into my hand. I grab the vial in one hand and the plastic hub in the other. Using my thumbs I flip the small blue caps off the end of each and screw them together. I then pull the protective cover from the needle point it up and push lightly on the vial until liquid squirts out. This maneuver is to get the air out so you don't inject a bubble into the patient's cardiovascular system. Movies and TV make it look as if one little bubble in an IV will kill someone, this is an urban legend. While it takes a fair amount of air to actually cause someone trouble medical personnel do make every effort to not inject air into a patient no matter how small the amount.

I grab for an alcohol pad and tear it open with my teeth. I rub it on the rubber injection port in the IV line. I then push the needle on the vial of lidocaine into the injection port. Shirley crimps off the line and I slowly push the medication into the patient's blood stream. All the time I am looking at the monitor and the patient to see if there are any unwanted reactions to the medication. It takes about a minute to give all the lidocaine. Just as I expected, her heart rate drops to a more normal 80 beats per minute. We have now done everything we can do for her it's now time to get to the hospital.

"Betty, go get the stretcher. Shirley, get a blood pressure while I hang the drip."

As I get the drip ready I ask the family which hospital they want her to go to. You would normally go to the closest but we are about equal distance to two capable of handling a post full arrest patient.

"Her doctor's in Conroe so let's go there," they tell me.

I keep a constant eye on the patient making sure her color is good, her respirations are ok, and heart rate stable.

I think. *Now I just hope she doesn't have brain damage.*

Betty returns with the stretcher maneuvering it up next to the patient. I hear a moan and realize it came from the patient. We all look at her and see her head moving slightly from side to side, all good signs.

Betty kneels by her and calls her by name, "Nancy, Nancy, can you hear me?"

Nancy doesn't actually respond to Betty's question but does continue to moan and move her head.

"Let's get her on the stretcher. Betty grab her head and shoulders. Shirley you get her legs."

I grab her midsection and wait for Betty to give the cadence. The person at the patients head always gives the cadence, that is, counts to three so everyone can lift together. Betty gets hold under the patient's shoulders looks to see if Shirley and I are ready.

"One, two, three, go," She says as we all lift the patient about a foot and a half off the floor and place her on the stretcher. We quickly seat belt her in and head for the ambulance.

"Betty can you ride with us to the hospital, just in case she goes out again?" I ask.

"Do you think she is going to make it? Betty asked as we start out.

"Well her vitals are stable her heart rate's good and she's moving and moaning. That's more than we've had on any other full arrest we've worked together isn't it?" I say with a smile.

In reality up to this moment I had only had one full arrest patient regain a heartbeat and that only lasted for about five minutes.

"You know you are the reason for her doing so good. It was a witnessed arrest and you started CPR immediately, which made the difference."

By the time we get to the emergency room the patient is responding to her name but still not fully awake. Over the next several days Betty keeps in contact with the hospital and family checking on her condition. The patient steadily improves and is able to walk out of the hospital 10 days later with no apparent brain damage.

Betty kept track of this patient until she moved away and we know for a fact she lived at least 10 more years.

Just Curious

Shirley and I walk into the front door of a large well-furnished two story house. Two first responders from the local fire department informed us by radio prior to arrival that they are assisting with respirations on a 45 year old woman. Robert, one of the first responders, is standing at the top of the sweeping staircase.

"Up here," he tells us.

When we reach the top of the stairs, he starts walking toward the patient and telling us what has happened.

"Her breathing's gotten very shallow since we got here we are assisting her with the   bag valve mask. Her kid came home from school and found her unconscious on the bedroom floor and called for help. We think she took too many Darvocets. The kid says she refilled the pills yesterday and about 20 of them are missing. Says her mother has some kind of medical problem that caused her a bunch of pain. Says she gets to hurting and takes more that she should sometimes."

"How's her heart rate and blood pressure?" I ask.

"Pressure's OK. Heart's a little slow, running about 50 to 60 beats per minute," answers Jim.

"Let's get her on the monitor," I say to no one in particular as I set monitor down and turn it on.

Shirley has already relieved Jim and is now assisting respirations. I tell Jim to go get the scoop stretcher. I unzip the bag attached to the monitor and take out the sealed package that contains the electrodes. I open it and apply them to the patient's upper right and left shoulders and lower left chest. I then snap the wires from the monitor to the electrodes. The heart rhythm is normal but slower than Jim said it was.

"Jim, get another BP for me Ok."

In a few seconds Jim tells me the patient's blood pressure has dropped to 88 over 60.

"Was she responsive at all when you got here?"

"No."

Her daughter is in the room, so I ask her the same question. The daughter informs me her mother was unresponsive when she got home. I do a sternum rub to see if she is responsive to pain.

When you are dealing with an unconscious patient a good paramedic attempts to determine how unconscious they are. Some patents while unconscious will respond when you call their name loudly and might even open their eyes or attempt to move if you ask them to. If the patient doesn't respond to verbal stimuli the next step is to see if they will respond to painful stimuli. There are several ways to do this. The most popular being the sternum rub. You take your knuckles and rub up and down on the patient's sternum, starting out lightly you increasing pressure on the sternum until you get a response from the patient or determine they are not going to respond. It takes a lot of pressure to get her to moan just a little. I know she is in bad shape and her vitals are deteriorating as we watch.

"We need to get going," I tell the others as Robert returns with the scoop stretcher.

Robert lays the scoop on the floor next to the patient. There is a latch at the head and foot of a scoop that separates it into two halves. We then place each half on either side of the patient. The halves are then pushed back together and locked. The patient is cradled to some extent making it much easier to move them out of an area where a regular stretcher won't fit. We use it quite often to get patients out of bathrooms, small bedrooms, and down stairs.

Shirley continues to ventilate the patient as Jim, Robert, and I maneuver her down the stairs. It's not that the patient weighed that much, it's that most houses are not designed with the thought of getting people around and out of them in a wheel chair or a stretcher. The stairs in this house are only wide enough for one person. Getting down them without dropping her, keeping her somewhat level, and continuing to ventilate her takes team work and communications between all four of us. We finally get to the bottom of the stairs and place her on the stretcher which Robert had thoughtfully brought in with him when he got the scoop stretcher.

"Well that was fun," I say breathlessly, as I look around and see the others are also trying to catch their breath.

"It could be worse," exclaims Jim. "The air conditioner could be broken." We all exchange glances as we roll the patient to the ambulance.

"Jim, could you relieve me on ventilations?" ask Shirley.

They switch as I take another blood pressure and reassess the patient's level of consciousness. After several sternum rubs it's clear she is now completely unresponsive to painful stimuli. Her blood pressure is now 80/56, not good.

"OK, I'm going to intubate her before we roll."

I quickly gather the equipment I need to get this done. I visualize the patient's vocal cords and pass the ET tube into her trachea between shallow breaths. I quickly start an IV. With Jim riding along and Shirley driving we head to the hospital. I open the medication cabinet and select the Narcan, a drug used to counteract drug overdoses. While it's intended to be used for opiate overdoses it also works but less effectively on other pain medications like Darvon.

While I hurry to give the patient the Narcan through her IV, I watch the monitor and see her heart rate fall and suddenly stop in a matter of 30 seconds or so. Jim is still ventilating her as I reach for her carotid artery to check for a pulse knowing I won't find one.

"Did we lose her?" asks Jim.

"Yes."

The monitor is showing a variation of Pulse less Electrical Activity that some paramedics call "dead with bumps". The complexes on the screen are very wide and rounded off instead of the sharp peaks usually associated with a normal rhythm or PEA. I start one hand chest compressions and tell Shirley to radio the hospital and let them know we now have a full arrest. With the other hand I reach for the epinephrine the first drug of choice for PEA. Jim continues to ventilate the patient every 4 or 5 chest compressions as I tear the box open with my teeth. I have now done as much as I can with one hand.

"Jim, take over compressions for a second."

As I move over a little Jim shifts his position so he can put one hand on her chest and still squeeze the BVM with the other. I pop the tops on the vial and needle holder and screw them together. Pinching the IV line so the epinephrine goes into the patient and not up into the IV bag I start to give the medication. As I do this I automatically look at the heart monitor to see if there is going to be any reaction. I am surprised to see what looks like sinus rhythm in between the chest compressions. I stop giving the epinephrine and tell Jim to stop compressions. Sure enough sinus rhythm. I quickly check for a pulse and yes she has one.

"Ok, Jim she's got a pulse back keep ventilating her."

I then turn my attention to the front of the ambulance, "Shirley, call the hospital back and let them we got a pulse back."

"We're only a few blocks away, by the time I raise them on the radio we'll be there," Shirley informs me.

"Did the epinephrine bring her around?" asks Jim.

"I don't think I gave her enough to do much of anything. The only thing I can think of is that the Narcan finally kicked in."

As we move the patient onto the hospital bed I quickly fill the ER doctor in as to what had happened up to that point.

"Give her another dose of Narcan," he tells the head nurse.

In a few moments she is giving the patient another round of the narcotic antagonist. Almost immediately the patient starts moving her head along with chewing on the ET tube. The respiratory therapist quickly removes the ET tube as the patient continues to rapidly regain consciousness. I wait a few more minutes and by then the patient is responding to her name. We are all quite pleased with ourselves knowing we had brought this person back. As we leave the trauma room the doctor tells us we did a good job.

A few days later I get a phone call.

"Are you Patrick Ramsey?" the male voice on the other end asks.

"Yes, I am"

"I was given your number by the dispatcher. She said you were the paramedic that took care of my wife the other day."

"What is your wife's name?" I ask making sure he is who he says he is.

He gives me the right name and I ask him why he has called.

"Well my wife's chest is sore. We were wondering if you had to do CPR on her the other day?"

I would have thought the hospital would have told him but it seems they didn't.

"Yes sir we did have to do CPR for a few minutes but the medication I gave her finally kicked in and it started again."

"That means that she was dead for a few minutes doesn't it?" he stutters.

"Well yes, technically she was, but she didn't do without oxygen and from what I understand she is going to make a complete recovery."

As a paramedic you rarely get a patient or their family calling you. On the rare occasion they do it is usually to thank you. Since the husband had specifically asked about his wife dying I assume he called to thank us for saving her. I was wrong.

"Well we were just wondering why her chest was sore," he tells before hanging up.

Like I said people rarely thank you.

Chapter 7....For Sale Cheap...
One Life...

What is a life worth? A question for which there is no answer. Is it how much a person will earn in their lifetime? Is it the actual worth of the chemicals and elements in your body? Is it how much they were loved, or how much they loved others? There is no correct answer. I bring this up because people die and are killed for little of nothing. It is what most of us call "A senseless death."

Anytime a life is taken it is a tragedy. These stories are an example of some of the more senseless deaths I have seen.

No Use Crying Over Spilled Beer

It's Saturday about 1:00 A.M. in Navasota Texas. Its early fall, about the time of the year when it actually starts to cool off after midnight. I had only been in bed a few minutes when the pager goes off. The worst time to get up is when you have only been asleep for a few minutes. It was one of those calls that started out bad and went downhill from there.

The pager comes to life and the friendly voice of the dispatcher tells us to respond to an unknown type call at Navasota Manor. Navasota Manor is one of two low income government apartment projects in this small town. The other apartment project named Navasota Village was on the opposite side of town. After clearing the call with the dispatcher Mike and I head for Navasota Manor. A minute or so later the dispatcher realizes she has sent us to the wrong apartment complex.

"Dispatch to Medic nine," she calls.

"Medic nine," I reply.

"Medic nine the call is at Navasota Village not Navasota Manor."

"Medic nine clear on Navasota Village, We are turning around," I tell her.

"Wonder if she has any idea as to what kind of call it is," Mike says as he makes a u turn.

"I'll ask but I'm willing to bet you a dollar she doesn't have any more information," I say.

"Not going to take that bet 'cause I'll lose for sure," Mike jokes back.

I ask anyway and just as predicted all she can tell us is that a police officer on the scene had requested an ambulance. During all of this conversation back and forth on the radio the officer on the scene never broke in and said anything. In a minute I would find out why.

About an hour earlier at a rundown bar in town two young men, one 16 years old and the other 20, both too young to even be in a bar, had gotten into an argument over a spilled beer. After arguing for a while the 16 year old decided to head for home. The 20 year old followed him out and the argument continued while they and a couple of other fellow drinkers walked the mile or so to the apartment complex. Witnesses said the 16 year old, one of the star football players at the local high school, finally tired of arguing turned and walked away. Moments later the 20 year old pulled a butcher knife and stabbed the 16 year old in the neck. The knife which entered the back of his neck just to the left of the spinal column severed his internal and external carotid artery, the jugular vein, and went through his larynx. The exit wound was in the front of his neck just below the larynx. He could not have been saved from this wound even if a surgeon had been standing next to him. He was more than likely dead within 15 or 20 seconds.

The call to 911 only requested a police officer. He arrived on the scene and quickly called for an ambulance forgetting or being too excited to explain why.

The complex covers about three blocks and is made up of one story buildings with four apartments in each building. Mike turns into the main entrance of the complex. Both of us are completely unprepared for what we have just driven into. A large crowd of at least 100 people is in the parking lot. All of them seem to be yelling and screaming at the same time. I look for the police officer that is on the scene and finally spot him standing in the middle of the crowd.

Mike finally expresses what we are both thinking, "Looks like we drove into the middle of a riot doesn't it?"

"That's what makes this job fun, the unknown. Speaking of the unknown wonder where our patient is?" I comment back.

Since the crowd is centered around Ralph, the police officer, we assume that is where the patient is. We have assumed right, as soon as the crowd notices us about half of them start waving and pointing in that direction.

"Sure would have been nice for Ralph to tell us what we were getting into," Mike says.

"Yea it would, maybe he's too busy," I say sarcastically.

Amid angry shouts for us to hurry up, Mike and I have to practically fight our way through the crowd to the patient. Mike is just in front of me as we get to the center of the mob. The crowd is pressed in so close we are practically on top of the patient before we see him. He is face down on the side walk. A huge puddle of blood is around the upper part of his body. Mike being in front me kneels down to check the patient. The crowd is now pressing in even more than before. Not knowing what we have gotten ourselves into and being in the middle of a hostile crowd, I decide to stand over Mike as he checks the patient. I figure I can hold them off long enough for him to get to his feet if the crowd turns on us.

I quickly glance at Ralph and see the fear in his face. This strikes me as funny since he is a police officer and the only one with a gun, except for possibly some of the people in the crowd.

As Mike checks for a pulse I hear a voice in the crowd yell a question.

"Is he dead? Is he dead? Cause if he's dead there's gonna be some white m----- f------ die tonight."

Since there were only three white people present at the time, Mike, Ralph, and myself I took this threat rather seriously. For the first time in my career I actually feared for my life for a few moments. Mike and I both knew the patient was dead. We also felt that telling the angry crowd he was dead meant we might be next.

While we were fighting our way through the mob several of them opened the back doors of the ambulance and actually managed to get the stretcher out and drag it up to the patient. Seeing this, Mike thinks quickly and comes up with an idea that probably kept us out of harm's way.

He turns to the men who have dragged the stretcher to us and says, "Guys if you want us to help him help us get him to the ambulance."

With that said several of them pick up the patient and lay him on the stretcher and start rolling it toward the ambulance. Mike and I follow still not knowing how or why he had been killed. As I fight my way back through the mob I look over to the ambulance and see several people beating the sides of it with their fist. Our "helpers" get to the ambulance and in their attempt to put the stretcher into the ambulance almost drop the body on the ground. After fighting with it for a second or two they finally get it in. Mike gets in the back and I make a run to the driver's side door. I remembered being told by some Houston paramedics that they had actually had their ambulance stolen in similar situations. Someone in the crowd being anxious to get the patient to the hospital actually jumps in and drives the ambulance themselves. Not wanting this to happen to us I make a beeline for the door and jump in.

I shout back through the walkway, "Are you ready Mike?"

"Let's get out of here," he says.

My plan is to get out of the area quickly. I pull the shift lever into drive and look up to see people running back and forth in front of the unit. They are yelling at me to go but won't get out of the way. At the risk of making them angrier I blip the siren and start to move. As I pass by them, several take swings at the windshield and sides of the unit. I inch my way past them and finally get clear. I turn on to the main road and realize that the other police officers in town and dispatcher do not know what's going on. Ralph in his state of fear has yet to use the portable radio he is carrying to let anyone else know that a riot is brewing. I decide to tell them.

I key the radio and call for the dispatcher, she answers quickly.

"Dispatch, are you aware that we have a riot at our location involving at least 100 people?"

Before she has time to answer the two other officers on duty that night radio they are responding.

I then call the hospital emergency room on the cell phone and quickly tell the charge nurse that we are bringing them a dead body. I give her a short explanation about the situation and that for our safety we had no choice. Being a small hospital they know Mike and I personally and realize we would not be doing this unless it was necessary.

Meanwhile back at the projects the other officers arrive to find Ralph sitting in his patrol car. Part of the mob is hanging around the puddle of blood. Another part of it, relatives and friends of the patient, have left to go to the hospital. Another group of about 20 have cornered the assailant in an empty apartment and are beating him up. The two officers that have just arrived, Kim and Craig, are told the crowd found the murderer hiding in the apartment. They make their way down to where he is to find him cowered on the floor with about 20 people attempting to kick and hit him.

They are ignored when they order everyone to leave him alone and get out of the apartment. Even when they start pulling people off of him they go right back to beating him. Having no

161

other choice they use pepper spray on anyone within range. Gradually they thin the crowd and find the murderer happy to be arrested. As the officers start out the door they realize their patrol cars are about half a block away. The crowd including the ones they pepper sprayed on are now waiting for them to bring him out. Not wanting to run the gauntlet to the cars they had hoped Ralph would come to help them. To their surprise he has left the scene and they are forced to push and shove their way to the patrol cars.

Meanwhile back at the hospital I back up to the emergency room door and we quickly take the young man into the trauma room. The nurses and doctor on duty are full of questions ranging from who he is to how he got stabbed. Unfortunately we have few answers.

Suddenly a crowd of people that consist of family and friends are banging on the emergency room door. Luckily the large metal door that is the ambulance entrance and the only way into the hospital at that time of night is locked. Being a small rural hospital it does not have security. While they banged on the door I grab the phone and call the police dispatcher and inform her that the riot or at least part of it has moved to the hospital and we need assistance.

Travis, a Texas highway patrol officer who was just coming into town to assist with the riot is passing the hospital when the dispatcher puts out our call for help. Travis is your stereo typical Texan. Well over six feet tall with a heavy built he pulls into the parking lot and walks right into the middle of the crowd. Immediately the family of the patient demands to be let into the hospital. He agrees to let the immediate family in. He goes to the door and the nurse lets them in while the rest of the crowd continues to carry on outside.

Kim and Craig are pulling up to the back door of the police station with the prisoner when they hear the call for help at the hospital. The dispatcher hits the buzzer and lets them in the back door to the jail. They find the nearest cell, throw him in and head out to assist us. As they head out to help at the hospital, Craig tells the dispatcher to not let anyone in the building fearing the some of the crowd might try to lynch the prisoner.

In the trauma room the doctor, Mike, and I are checking the body. In the rush to get him and ourselves out of a bad situation we had not had time to see all of his wounds. We still didn't know why he had been stabbed or who did it. Mike and I check his pockets to try to find some kind of identification while the doctor probes the stab wound to see what organs the knife damaged. Mike finds a key ring with one of those little plastic tags on it. The tags inscription says "I'm proud of my bad ass attitude" a prophetic epitaph considering why he was killed.

Later that night as I talked with the family of the patient, I found out his older brother was the person who made the threat of killing Mike and me if his brother was dead. He went on to explain that he had had another brother stabbed to death in Houston and was angry that it had happened again. While he offered an explanation he never did apologize for saying it. To this day I still don't understand his statement. Mike and I were there to try to help and because of the color of our skin we were threatened. If a white person had stabbed him, I might have understood but that was not the case.

Travis, Craig, and Kim were finally successful in getting the crowd to leave the hospital. Ralph disappeared for the rest of the night and ended up quitting the police department the next day.

Many months later I ran across Ralph and had a chance to talk to him about the incident for the first time. He admitted to me that he had never been so scared in his life and froze unable to do his job. While it was a difficult situation and I did have some serious concern for Mike and my safety we did what had to be done. If we had froze as he did our careers as paramedics would have been over. He however was able to get a job as a constable out in the country where he hoped he would not have to deal with anything like that again.

Just think of it. A young man killed, a riot, damage to our ambulance, a police officer gets scared and quits, all because of a spilled beer.

Hey, Man My Beer's Getting Hot

It's early Saturday afternoon, and it's the middle of summer in south east Texas. A crisis has developed at a rental home. The air conditioner has stopped working. One of the three young men that live there calls the landlord and informs him of the situation. In turn the landlord calls a personal friend who repairs air conditioners and asks him to go take a look.

The AC man arrives on the scene and starts to work on the unit. Before he goes up into the attic of the old wood frame house to check that part of the system he does what all good AC men do. He goes to the circuit breaker box and turns off the electricity.

Meanwhile the three men and their girlfriends are outside playing Frisbee. We all know playing Frisbee on a hot summer day can make you very thirsty, before long one of the men head into the house to "get a cold one." When he opens the refrigerator door he notices the light is not on. Panic sets in at the thought of his beer getting warm. He storms out of the house to the breaker box. With only one thought in mind, save the beer, he turns the electricity back on.

He resumes the game knowing his party won't be ruined by warm beer. Half an hour passes and one of the others makes the comment that they have not heard from nor seen the AC man for about an hour. Not seeing him outside they check in the house and finally look in the attic.

They find him slumped over the AC unit. In a brief moment of intelligence the man who turned the electricity back on realizes what he has done and runs down to turn the breakers off. None of them attempt to check the AC man or get him out of the attic.

I arrive on the scene just after the first responders have gotten him out of the attic and started CPR. It's clear that he's a young man so I start looking for signs of injury that would cause his heart to stop. Knowing I will put the patient on the cardiac monitor the first responders have already cut his shirt up the front.

I see what looks like a burn about 8 inches long running across his upper abdomen. I see no other signs of injury. I know he was found in the attic because the first responders had radioed and told me. Other than that we know nothing about how or why he is in cardiac arrest.

I turn on the monitor/defibrillator pull the paddles from their cradle and get ready to check his heart rhythm. It takes a moment for the screen to light up so I decide to try and get some information from the three men sitting calmly on the couch.

"Do any of you know what happened?" I ask.

"No man, we just found him like that and called for the ambulance," they lied.

"What was he doing in the attic?"

"Listen man we don't know nothing. He just came here to work on the air conditioner."

It becomes obvious they are not going to tell us anything. It also becomes fairly obvious that the burn on his abdomen is probably caused by electricity and that he has been electrocuted.

"Stop compressions." I say as I place the paddles on the patient chest.

The first responder stops compressions and withdraws just a bit in anticipation of me defibrillating him. I hold the paddles still with a steady pressure so as to get an accurate reading. The horizontal yellow line stays just as straight as it had been before I put the paddles on his chest. No activity at all, straight line, as we call it.

Contrary to what you see on TV and in the movies it doesn't do any good to defibrillate a heart that has no electrical activity. I put the paddles away and tell the first responder to continue CPR. At that moment one of the men on the couch says something I will never forget.

"Listen man, if the son of a bitch is dead just leave him alone."

We all hear him say it and give each other a look of disbelief as we continue to work on the patient. I have no idea how long ago the patient's heart stopped but suspect it has been at least 20 minutes. I had no way of knowing at the time it had been at least an hour. I know there is no hope to resuscitate him but protocols, at that time, said we had to continue CPR once it had been started.

My partner, Keith, knowing I will intubate the patient next, has already gotten the kit out. I select a 7.5 mm tube and a number three Macintosh blade for the laryngoscope. There are two basic types of blades used to intubate a patient. The Macintosh is slightly curved and the miller blades are basically straight. Each medical professional has his or her own preference as to which blade they like to use. I prefer the Macintosh, probably because that was the one preferred by the doctor that taught me to intubate.

I hold the laryngoscope in my left hand and put the blade into the patient's mouth until it stops against at the back of his throat. There is a small bright light near the end of the blade that lights up the patient's throat. I lift up and away a few inches, this causes the patients head to fall back and the neck to arch and open the airway. The blade also holds up the patient's tongue. As the head falls back the epiglottis is pulled away from the larynx and I should be able to see the patient's vocal cords. After I see the vocal cords I pass the ET tube past them a couple of inches. I have to be careful here because if you go too far the tube goes beyond the trachea and into the right lung. I see the tube go in, holding it with my right hand I remove the laryngoscope.

I look up and my partner has the BVM ready. He attaches it to the end of the ET tube and squeezes it forcing air into the patient's lungs. I listen with a stethoscope to make sure air is going into the patient's lungs. I hear air go into both lungs. With tape I secure the tube so it will not come out. The whole operation takes less than a minute.

"Continue CPR," I tell the first responders.

They resume CPR as my partner hard wires the patient to the cardiac monitor. He is still in asystole, *Big surprise*, I think.

The fact that the air conditioner is not working has become evident. All of us working the patient are now ringing wet with sweat. I know the patient has no hope and since we cannot stop CPR I decide to go ahead and get the patient to the ambulance.

I look up and tell Randy, one of the firsts responders, to get the back board and stretcher. He takes off and the rest of us start getting ready to move the patient. My partner starts throwing equipment back into the trauma bag. One of the first responders and I tie the patient's hands together. If you don't secure an unconscious person's arms they will get in the way. It is embarrassing to roll a patient out the door with their arms hanging off the sides of the stretcher and getting caught in the door jam. After having this happen a couple of times I learned to secure them.

Randy is attempting to make his way through the front door pushing the stretcher with the backboard on top. He is having some trouble getting it over the threshold and asks for someone to give him a hand. The three of us are busy and under normal circumstances you would expect one of the three young men enjoying the show to get up and help, they don't.

I look directly at the one that mouthed off about leaving him alone and say. "You, get up and help him!" He gives me one of those, who me, looks and I tell him in no uncertain terms. "Get up and get the door, now!"

He reluctantly gets up, takes a few steps to the door and throws it open and immediately sits back down. Randy makes it to where we are and, following a routine we had been through many times, grabs the backboard and lays it on the floor beside the patient. I am now ventilating the patient so I start to get everyone in position so we can effectively and quickly move the patient out of the sweat box we are in.

"Don, get his body. Keith, get the legs."

Don, who is doing chest compressions, stops reaches across the patient and grabs his shoulder and belt. Keith stops packing up the kits and knelling on the same side of the patient as Don grabs his thigh and calf. Randy is on the other side holding backboard with the edge of it touching the patient.

"Everybody ready?" I ask. Everyone shakes their head yes. "One two three roll."

Don and Keith quickly roll the patient onto his side while I stabilize his head and roll with them. At the same time Randy slides the board under his back.

"One two three, down," I count.

We roll him back centering him on the board. Don resumes chest compressions and Randy rolls the stretcher close to us. I am at the head so I get to lift that part of the backboard. Keith is at the feet so he gets to lift there. Randy and Don grab the sides of the backboard. I call the cadence and we pick up the patient and backboard placing it on the stretcher. Don and I resume CPR while the others secure the patient to the stretcher with seat belts.

"OK, let's get him to the unit," I say.

Sweat is now pouring off all of us, our shirts look like we have been standing in a shower. I ventilate with the BVM and Don does chest compressions while the other two push and pull the stretcher out the door and to the ambulance. None of the young men sitting on the couch bothers to get up and lend a hand during this operation.

Randy, waiting until we get outside to express his anger about the indifference of the young men in the house lets his opinion be known.

"What in the hell is wrong with those guys?" he ask to no one in particular. "If he's dead just leave the son of a bitch alone. Can you believe he said that?" he yells. "The stupid lazy bastards find him in the attic and then leave him there until we get here. How stupid can people be?" he says in frustration.

"Yea, I hear ya, if it wasn't for the extra paper work I'd have to fill out I would've strangled him then and there," I say jokingly trying to get Randy to calm down. I get a chuckle out of him as we lift the stretcher into the ambulance and lock it in.

I know that all of us feel the same way about what we have just witnessed but as with similar calls like this there is little we can do about it. Taking care of the patient even though he has no chance needs to be our focus.

"Keith, take over ventilations, I've got to wipe some of this sweat off," I say reaching for the cabinet that contains the towels.

I wipe my face and place it around my neck. I hand one to Keith and he does the same thing. Even though the ambulance is air conditioned the cool air escaped while we loaded the patient.

"Randy can you ride in with us?" I ask.

I need the extra help since trying to do one man CPR in the back of moving ambulance and give drugs to the patient is next to impossible.

"Sure," he says immediately.

"Where are the cops?" Keith asks.

"I don't see them," I reply. "We need to get going. Don would you wait for them and let them know what happened? I don't think they are telling us the whole story. I think the cops need to check it out."

Don agrees to stay.

Before we roll out, I attempt to get an IV but the patient has been down so long his veins have collapsed. I give the patient epinephrine down the ET tube, you do this if you can't get an IV, it's the next best way for the drugs to be absorbed.

"Come on AC," I say to anyone listening.

172

The towel draped around my neck is now as wet as my shirt.

Randy being funny says, "It'll cool off now that we are moving."

Like me he knows full well that patient compartment will barely cool down by the time we get to the hospital.

"Yea sure, we'll have the chills by the time we there," I answer sarcastically.

I give the patient a few more rounds of drugs during transport and, as expected, he remains in asystole.

We move the patient on to the hospital's stretcher. The emergency room doctor, seeing that the patient is young, does the same head to toe check that I had done earlier. He notices the bruising, which is now more visible that it was thirty minutes earlier.

"What in the hell caused this?" he demands.

I quickly fill him to the extent of what we know and saw, including the comment made by the man living in the house.

"He actually said that?" questions the doctor in disbelief.

"Yes he did, a real humanitarian," I tell him.

After cleaning up the ambulance we head back to the scene so Randy can get his car. As the house comes into view we see the three men and women playing Frisbee in the front yard.

Randy getting worked up again says, "Can you believe that? A man dies in their attic. They leave him there then tell us to leave him alone and they are out playing Frisbee like nothing happened."

Keith pulls in front of the house. Randy, afraid he will say something he regrets to the men, makes the wise decision to head straight for his car and leave. It is a good decision because I almost lose it when the man who told us to leave him alone if he was dead stops playing Frisbee comes over to the ambulance.

"How's the dude doin' man?" he asks.

I can smell the beer on his breath. At last, I think, a touch of humanity. This thought was short lived.

"He didn't make it," Keith tells him.

"Too f------ bad man, I told you to leave him alone." With that said he turns around and continues his game.

Later that evening the deputy that finally made it to the scene calls me to ask some questions. He tells me about the man turning the power back on when he found the refrigerator off. I fill him in about the man possibly being in the attic an hour before anyone became concerned enough to check on him and the comment made about leaving him alone.

"Are any charges going to be filed?" I ask.

"Probably not. We don't think there was any criminal intent. More than likely it will be ruled an accident," he tells me.

"Too bad you can't charge people with stupidity." I tell him getting upset with the idea that a man was killed because someone was afraid his beer would get warm.

Chapter 8....Hey, This Paramedic Stuff Really Works!

As I have said only a small percentage of EMS calls are actually life threatening. These are stories where patients were literally only a few minutes from dying when we arrived. Had it not been for the advanced equipment, medications, and training of my partner and myself these people would not have made it to the hospital alive.

Fish Boy

Jason and I are staged in the bank parking lot in Anderson. This staging point is roughly in the center of the county. We have two units that cover the entire county. One is stationed in the north part of the county the other is stationed near Navasota in south county. When one ambulance goes on a call the other unit moves to the staging point so as to be, at least in theory, equal distance to all points in the county. It's late autumn and the night air is cool so we have the windows rolled down and the AC turned off. We are talking and as usual solving the problems of the world.

"But I tell you a Whooper is better than a Quarter Pounder. They put mayonnaise on it. That makes any hamburger better."

Before Jason has a chance to reply dispatch calls us on the radio. Within a few moments we are heading to an unknown medical emergency in a van outside a house at Four Corners, a major intersection a few miles north of where we are located.

We spot someone flagging us down as we near our destination. Jason, in an effort to get in the last word tells me, "Ok I'll admit I like mayonnaise on a burger too but McDonalds will put it on for you if you ask."

Jason stops behind an old custom painted van, what used to be called a "Good Times Van." There are several people standing around the open right front door. I walk quickly to the door and find a young man reclined in the seat. In that first few seconds I take a survey of the scene and the patient. I notice his skin color is bright red, he is unconscious, and his breathing is labored and very shallow. Jason is right behind me with the kit and without saying a word puts him on high flow oxygen.

I shake him and only receive a moan in response. A young woman standing near starts to tell us what happened.

"He ate fish for supper and started to itch like crazy. Then he couldn't breath too good and ask us to take him to the hospital. I didn't think he was that bad so we started to drive to St. Joes. He quit talking to us in Iola so we found this house with the lights on and pulled in here to call for an ambulance."

Her quick story just confirmed what Jason and I suspected was wrong with the patient when we first saw him, anaphylactic shock. It is a severe allergic reaction that can kill a patient if left untreated. I grab his wrist checking his pulse, it's weak and irregular.

"Is he allergic to fish?" Jason asks the woman.

"He said he was but didn't think it was that big of a deal and ate it anyway."

Jason turns to the woman in disbelief, "You're telling me he knew he was allergic to fish and ate it anyway."

"Yea, he thought he would become less allergic if he ate more of it," answers the woman.

"Jason, get the stretcher. Let's get him loaded."

It only takes a few moments to get "Fish Boy", as Jason and I later named him, into the unit. His breathing has become so shallow by this time you can hardly see his chest move. I now have one of those split second decisions to make as far as treatment. Give him epinephrine either by IV or under the skin or attempt to intubate him. Intubating would be difficult if not impossible at this point because his throat is swollen. Epinephrine under this skin or sub-q as it is called might take several minutes to take effect. I decide to start an IV and give the epinephrine that way. If I can get the IV quickly, it will be the most effective way to give the medication.

Jason has already started assembling the IV bag and tubing. I put a tourniquet on his arm and find a vein. Working quickly, I tape the IV down as Jason gets the epinephrine ready. According to our protocols, I'm supposed to give him .3 mg of epinephrine to start with and another .3 if there is no change. I decide I don't have time for that. His reaction is so acute I know from experience he will need at least .5 of epinephrine before I will see a change. Jason pinches off the line and I push .5 into the patient's vein.

"Get the intubation kit out just in case this doesn't work," I tell Jason.

We know the epinephrine will work within a few seconds but the side effect of it is a rapid heartbeat. That is why you have to be careful to give enough to work but not too much. If you give too much you can send your patient's heart into V-tach, a potentially life threatening arrhythmia. Then you've created another problem you have to try to correct. I get the Benadryl from the drug box as "Fish Boy" starts to take deeper breaths. The Benadryl is to relieve the symptoms of allergic reactions specifically the itching and rash. I give him 50 mgs also through the IV.

"I think he's out of the woods. Let's go ahead and head for the hospital. Tell the family he's alright," Jason nods his head and goes out the side door.

As we head for the hospital "Fish Boy" continues to improve and after about 15 minutes he starts to come around enough to ask and answer questions.

"Where am I? What happened?" are his first questions.

"You're in an ambulance heading for the hospital. You had a severe reaction to the fish you ate. I understand you already knew you were allergic to fish?" I needed to know if what his friend told us was true about him being allergic to fish.

"Yea, I thought it would go away the more I ate."

I normally don't lecture my patients but I realize he didn't seem be aware how close he came to killing himself.

"Listen to me. You can never eat fish again. The reaction will get worse each time you eat it. You came within a few minutes of dying tonight. You are lucky your friends stopped when they did and we were nearby. Do you understand me?"

He shakes his head yes but I still wonder if he really understands.

The last time I saw him was as we left the emergency room. I heard the nurse giving him the same lecture I had about how he would die if he ate fish again. Hope he listened to us.

Having Fun in a State Prison

"I hate making prison calls!" This is something I said every time we had to go to the state prison in our territory. At one time the Texas Department of Corrections had an ambulance at almost all their prisons with medics just sitting around waiting for something to do. It was determined that a lot of money could be saved if they quit doing this and used the local EMS for emergency patients. I really didn't mind taking care of the prisons. What I did mind was dealing with the guards and the overall hassle of going into and out of the place. The main problem, as far as I was concerned, was the way guards treat everyone as if they are inmates including us.

We pull up to the main entrance. It consists of two heavy duty chain link gates placed about 100 feet apart, it's called the "sally port." The guard opens the first gate. We drive in and he is closes it behind us.

"Whut y'all here for?" asks the young guard trying to sound official.

"We're here to sell cigarettes to the prisoners and take the ones out that want to go," I say in a serious tone.

Somewhere is the back of his one track brain he realizes I am being a smart ass and manages a crooked smile. He's like most guards and just does a cursory look inside the unit before opening the second gate and letting us into the compound.

Mike and I know the way to the infirmary. During the day we enter the prison by the back door, so to speak. It's the entrance all the prisoners use to reenter the prison after working outside all day. It you get there right at quitting time there are hundreds of inmates lined up waiting their turn to be searched and take a shower. To make things easier for the guards the inmates strip while outside and throw theirs cloths into several large hampers as they wait to be checked in. Once in the showers are right there as you entered the door.

A young female EMT who was filling in for my regular partner ended up refusing to ride the ambulance in that district because she got an eye full one day. We were dispatched to the prison at about the time I knew the inmates would be lined up. I warned her about this and told her to look straight ahead and not to make eye contact. Even though I had warned her, she was not prepared for the sight of several hundred men making no attempt to cover up once they saw my partner, a young attractive blond. As we walked through the shower area several cat calls were heard even though the guards did attempt to keep them quiet.

Once through the shower area we pass the prison laundry. I had always thought it was just a thing for the movies to show these gigantic prison laundries with rows of steam presses and washing machines the size of compact cars but it's not.

Mike stops and we grab the stretcher and oxygen. We usually didn't carry anything else in. The idea was to get the patient and get them out to the unit and treat them there without interference from prison medical staff.

I knock on the door of the infirmary to get the attention of the guard. He waits a moment before unlocking it. No sense in getting in a hurry they are only prisoners. As much as he was indifferent, the nurse on the other hand was extremely glad to see us. Standing by the exam room door she motions us over.

"He's in here and he looks like crap," Nora tells us as we enter the room.

She's not joking. Laying on the gurney was an extremely pale and sweaty 50 year old man. Most of the white prisoners were pale and pasty anyway but he was way beyond that and somewhat cyanotic. Mike and I both notice how bad he looks and exchange glances. I then spot the cardiac monitor. It shows a heart rate of 180 to 200. The other nurse, Betty, has an IV catheter in her hand and is holding the patients arm looking unsuccessfully for a vein. Looking relived we have arrived, she hands the catheter to Mike.

"Here you try. I can't find anything."

"How long has he been like this?" asks Mike as he takes the IV catheter from Betty.

"About an hour, you know how long it takes to get clearance to send someone out," responds Betty.

"What's his blood pressure?" I ask Nora.

"It's low, 80 over 50 the last time I took it."

Mike and I both know as did the nurses he was in bad shape and would have to be treated there in the infirmary. When your heart is beating that fast for that long it becomes unable to pump enough blood to the body. If uncorrected the heart will eventually fail and the patient will die.

"Mike you get the IV and I'll go get the Adenocard."

"I'll be here," he responds.

Adenocard is a drug specifically used to slow someone's heart down in a situation like this. We have only been carrying it for about a month and this will be the first time to actually give it to a patient. It is given in a very specific manner and if given properly it causes the patient's heart to stop for 5 to 10 seconds so it can reset itself and hopefully resume beating a much slower rate. It's safe because it is only effective for 20 seconds or so once you give it. Before Adenocard the only drug available was very dangerous to give. It could actually stop the heart or slow it down so much you had to give other drugs to speed it up again. The only other alternative was synchronized cardio version. This is where you actually shocked the patient, sometimes while they are conscious, so as to allow the heart to reset. It works most of the time but is very uncomfortable for the patient.

It takes me about two to three minutes to make the round trip to get to the ambulance get the drug kit and return. As I reenter the exam room with the drug kit Mike is taping down the IV. He has started it in the patients anticubical, which is in the bend of the elbow. When giving Adenocard it is imperative you establish the IV with a large catheter 18 gage or larger in a large vein close to the heart.

"How you doing? Are you having any chest pain?" I ask the patient.

"I don't really have pain. It's just that my heart feels like it is going to jump out of my chest cause it beatn' so fast. I feel weak too."

Mike speaks up, "We're going to give you some medicine in a minute that's should fix that. You just bear with us, Ok."

The patient nods his head.

I grab the Adenocard and draw it up in a syringe. Mike at the same time is drawing up 10 CC's of saline into another syringe to use as a flush. To get the medicine to the heart as quickly as possible you give it IV push as fast as you can, you then push it along with the flush. Since Adenocard only has a half life of about 10 to 15 seconds it has to be given this way to be effective. If you don't give it fast enough nothing happens.

I stick the needle into the rubber injection port closest to the patient on the IV tubing. Mike does the same with the other syringe.

Is this gonna to hurt?" asked the patient weakly.

"No, it won't hurt but you are going to feel kind a funny for a few seconds," I reply.

I didn't want to tell him the funny feeling would be his heart stopping for a few seconds.

Betty and Nora, knowing the patient is not doing well, are watching us closely although they really don't know what to expect.

"Ready?" I ask Mike pinching the line.

"Go for it."

I put my thumb on the plunger and push it as fast as it will let me. Mike follows by pushing the saline just as quickly. Our eyes jump to the monitor in hopes of watching the patient's heart stop for a few seconds. Since neither of us had given Adenocard before we were anxious to see if it really worked as we had been told. I also keep an eye on the patient to see his reaction. Five or six long seconds pass and I am staring to think we may have not given it correctly. All of a sudden the patient eyes roll back in his head as his neck arches back. The line on monitor goes flat. Mike and I know his heart will start again but we silently hold our breath and wait. Within six or seven seconds a much slower rhythm appears on the scope. The patients eyes come back to normal, his neck relaxes, and his color improves considerably.

"Man what a rush!" he exclaims.

The nurses see the instant improvement in the patient and are greatly impressed. "What was that stuff?" asked Nora.

"Adenocard," replies Mike.

"It doesn't matter what it's called. I call it a wonder drug," says Betty.

"How do you feel?" I asked the patient.

"Man I don't know what that stuff was but it sure does work. I feel fine. No more racing heart. Man it was like you turned on a switch or something. Just like that I was better," he says as he tries to snap his fingers.

After everyone gets over the miraculous cure we have just witnessed, we have the patient move to our stretcher as we prepare to transport him.

"Aw man, do I really have ta go to the hospital? I feel great now."

"I'm afraid so, they have to find out what caused your heart to beat so fast. We only treated you for now. It won't stop another attack," I explain.

Like any government entity the prison has a set procedure to follow. As we wait for the "paper work" so we can actually leave the prison with him, one of the guards starts to shackle him. First the leg irons then the chain that hooks around their waist and is connected to the leg irons. It is called the belly chain for obvious reasons. The belly chain has a ring in it. One of the prisoner's hands is cuffed. The cuffs are run through the ring and the other hand is locked into the other cuff. This greatly limits arm movement and makes it darn near impossible to run, which is the idea. It was common practice to not cuff the hand that had the IV. The guard would normally cuff the other hand, then lock the other side of the cuffs to the ring. This is what was done to this patient.

Paper work done and the guard assigned to ride with the patient is ready to go. Out we go through the laundry and the showers and into the unit. Everything is fine; the patient is stable and the guard riding with us is not the usual Barney Fife type we usually deal with.

Mike pulls up to the first gate of the sally port and the same young no common sense guard lets us in and closes it behind us. He opens the back door of the unit to make sure we are not smuggling anyone out. The patient and I are the only ones in back the guards always ride up in the cab.

186

"What's your name and number?" he asks in the most demanding voice he can muster.

As the patient answers, the guard notices that the arm with the IV is not cuffed and proceeds to have a fit.

"That prisoner's hand is goin' to have to be cuffed or he can't leave," he screams at me.

Copping an attitude right back I try to explain, "The IV is near his wrist you can't put the cuffs on it."

"Well you're gonna to have to take it out so we can cuff him proper."

"I am not taking the IV out. He needs it.

The guard then tries to intimidate me, something that is very difficult to do.

"I told you to take that damn IV out, now!"

I decide to bluff him. In a loud and stern voice I tell him.

"If I take it out YOU will become medically responsible for him and YOU will have to ride to the hospital with him and it will be YOUR fault if anything happens to him. Do you understand me?"

His face turns three shades of red as he turns on his heels and walks over to a telephone and dials a number. I am too far away to hear the conversation but he is gesturing wildly with his free hand as he explains his side of the story. He finally stops and listens for a few seconds before slamming the phone down. Face still red as a beet he quickly walks back to the ambulance door and grabs it.

"Have a nice f___in trip," he shouts as he slams the door with all the might his scrawny body can muster.

He stomps around to the other gate throws it open and signals Mike to come on out. I had called his bluff and won. In spite of Bubba trying to keep us locked in, the patient made it to the hospital without any problems.

Legally passing electrical current through someone's body

Whenever we obtained a new piece of equipment or medicine, as in the previous story, most paramedics can't wait to use it. It was always exciting when the circumstances of a call warranted the use of something new.

Karen and I walk into the old wood frame house, the kind that sits up on blocks instead of a solid foundation. As usual, in Grimes County, we are in the middle of nowhere. Kathy, a first responder, is bent over a very thin man lying crosswise on the couch. She looks up at us just as she finishes letting the air out of the blood pressure cuff.

"You take it," she says, handing me the stethoscope. "I don't think I heard it right."

"What did you get?" I ask.

Kathy, one of the best first responders I ever worked with, was sometimes a bit unsure of herself, especially if was different from what she expecting.

"I got 50 over 40 but I know that ain't right."

I look at the emaciated looking man who appears to be unconscious, whose breathing is very shallow and figure Kathy is probably close to being right.

I start squeezing the rubber bulb as Karen proceeds to ask questions in an effort to get some kind of a medical history on the man. I turn the silver knob and the air starts to escape from the cuff. I listen and watch the needle on the dial as it falls. Just as it gets to 50 I hear one beat. As it passes 40 I hear another beat. I pull the stethoscope out of my ears as Kathy asked me what I got.

"The same thing you did."

I could also tell his heart rate was very slow. I know I won't be able to feel a pulse on his wrist so I put my fingers on his neck to feel for the carotid pulse. I can only feel a beat every three seconds or so. That means his heart is only beating 20 times a minute. It should normally beat 60 to 70 times a minute.

"No wonder he's unconscious." I think.

"What kind of medical history does he have?" I asked Kathy.

"He just lives with these people. They kina just took him in. He is supposed to be a Vietnam Vet and have Agent Orange Syndrome." Kathy tells me as Karen hooks him up to the monitor.

I am not surprised when I see on the monitor he has a full heart block. In this case the block is in the electrical signal that goes through your heart and not a blocked artery. The electric impulse starts at the top of your heart and makes the small chambers known as the atrium beat. The signal then goes down and makes the ventricles beat. When that signal fails to make it to the ventricles they beat at their own rate which is 20 to 30 beats a minute. This is an arrhythmia that needs a pacemaker. Lucky for this patient our monitor is equipped with an external pacemaker. We've only had it a couple of month and I have been dying to try it out.

We quickly get him out to the ambulance. Kathy is setting up the IV while Karen looks for a vein. I open the $50.00 package that contains two special pads used with the external pacemaker function on the cardiac monitor. Karen gets the IV on the first try and I peel the backing off the pads. I place one on his upper right chest and the other on his lower left about 16 inches below his arm pit. There are wires already connected to the pads. They are about 6 feet long and have a special plug to hook them into the monitor.

"Are we going to pace him?" asked Karen.

"Yes, we are just as soon as you give him some atropine and it doesn't work, I am going to start pacing him."

Atropine is used to speed the heart up but it only works when it is just slow and not in a heart block. The reason for giving it is that our written protocol says we have to give it first and when it doesn't work then we can pace the patient.

Because the patient is unconscious Karen and I decide not to give him a drug called Versed, which causes amnesia. Kathy looks on anxiously as I set the rate at 70 beats per minute at minimal current. The objective is to gradually increase the current until you get capture. That is when the patient's heart starts to beat at 70 times a minute. Since you are passing current through their body as well as their heart the patient's upper body twitches 70 times a minute. It's an odd site the first time you see it.

I finally get capture when I see and feel a heartbeat after each pacemaker spike. In a few minutes his blood pressure is 90 over 60 and his skin color is better. He's still unconscious and remains that way until we get him to the hospital.

I call the emergency room and give them a report on our patient. I also make a point of telling them they need to have another pacemaker ready so we don't have to wait for them to find one.

"What do you want to bet they don't have one ready when we get there? What do you want to bet they don't believe he really needs a pacemaker and turn ours off to see what happens? Come on Kathy tell me."

"I won't bet against you. I know how they get," answers Kathy.

Yea, we all know how some of them get. While most emergency room nurse and doctors work well with the local EMS crews, there are a few that seem to resent the fact that paramedics can actually preform advance procedures before we arrive at the ER. They are quick to assume we don't know what we are doing or talking about. The nurse we happen to be dealing on this night has a reputation of being arrogant toward ambulance personnel.

"Put him over there," says nurse Crachet.

Pointing to one of the stretchers lined up in the general exam area.

"I knew it, she doesn't even think he's bad enough to put him in the cardiac room," I whisper to Karen.

"Where's the doctor?" I ask the nurse.

"Why do you need the doctor? Just tell me what's wrong with him and you can be on your way," she replies in the most arrogant voice she can muster.

"I already called and told y'all that I'm pacing this patient. I can't just stop and walk away. You know that."

"Yes, you can if I tell you to. I've been a nurse for 10 years."

"I've been a paramedic for 15 years . You can't tell me a damn thing. Now, go get the doctor."

I had raised my voice enough that the doctor heard me and suddenly appears at the patient's side. Before she has a chance to reply the doctor tells her to go get the pacemaker. Nurse Crachet turns on her heels and storms down to the trauma room to retrieve it.

We move the patient to the hospital stretcher. He is just starting to moan and groan another sign the pacemaker is doing its job.

"Ok, go ahead and turn to pacemaker off so we can see what's going to happen," the doctor tells us.

"I can tell you what's going to happen. He's going to go back to a heart rate of 20 and his blood pressure is going to drop," I tell him.

"Yea, I know but maybe he's not really in a heart block. Besides we have to turn it off so I can hook him up to ours."

I reach over and disable the pacemaker. Just as I predicted his heart rate drops back to 20 and his blood pressure bottoms out.

"Turn it back on until we get ours ready," says the doctor quickly.

I hit the switch but have to start the process of increasing the current, until I get capture, over again. By then the nurse is back with the hospital's pacemaker. She lays it down on the counter and walks away. The doctor picks it up and we quickly find out the connectors for the pacing pads are different and we just can't unplug and plug them back in to theirs. We are going to have to peel ours pads off and put theirs on.

With all this done and the patient finally being paced again the doctor starts asking if the patient's relatives are present. We explain the situation and point out the woman who's family he lives with.

Without introducing himself he starts asking her questions, "Is he a DNR patient?"

"A what?"

"You know. Do you want us to try to revive him if his heart stops?"

"Well of course we do. He's not that sick is he?"

"He's pretty bad. He's going to need to have an internal pacemaker put in. Do you think he would want that?"

"Well of course he would!" exclaims the friend.

Not being able to hold it in any longer I tell Karen and Kathy. "The compassion and love in this place is just overwhelming, I'm getting choked up. Let's go."

I go up to the nurses' station to get a copy of the patient's information. Nurse Crachett is there and wants to get the last word. "The next time you talk to me like that, I'll call your supervisor."

I lean over the counter and whisper. "You'll call and tell him what. That I was right and you're wrong. That every time I come in here you go out of your way to be an ass. By the way, see this white shirt? I am the supervisor."

"You can't talk to me like that."

"Why? You just talked to me like that. What's the difference?"

She knew there wasn't and suddenly found something else important to do.

Karen who had witnessed several arguments between me and nurse Crachett shakes her head and says, "You really like getting under her skin don't you?"

"Yes, I do. She is so used to bullying the other paramedics who come in here she thinks she can treat everyone that way. I finally got tired of putting up with her crap. She's all talk and no do. She knows she is out of line. Everybody else lets her get away with it, I don't."

I check in on my patient before I leave. Even though he is being paced, his condition is serious. He is still unresponsive. I leave the emergency room wondering, like the doctor, if he will make it.

Kathy saw the patient a month later. She called and told us that she didn't recognize him at first. He had gained some weight and was walking and talking. He had been rushed to emergency surgery later that night where an internal pacemaker was installed. He still had his other medical problems but the pacemaker that he apparently had needed for a while helped him return to a more normal life.

Two for One

David and I have been trying to find the little white wood frame house on the second dirt road off of County Road 43 for over 45 minutes. We have traveled from the station all the way across the county to a sparsely populated area in the eastern part. Due to the sparse population we rarely made calls in this area. Not knowing the area, poorly marked roads, and it being the middle of the night add to us taking nearly an hour to find the house.

We finally spot a teenage boy excitedly flags us down as we come to a stop in front of the dilapidate house. Dust swirls around the ambulance as David and I grab the usual equipment out of the back. Weeds and tall grass almost block the entrance. The boy leads us down a dark narrow path I finally take out my Mini Mag flash light so I can see where I'm going. Several planks are missing from the porch. The ones that are still there are rotten. David and I step carefully to avoid falling through.

"It'll be fun getting him out of here," whispers David as we get to the door. I nod in agreement.

"Here he is," says the boy.

He is pointing to a thin pale unconscious man lying on a worn out couch in the living room. As we walk towards the man a woman sitting in a matching worn out chair starts to tell us what has happened.

"He's a diabetic. I think his sugars low. He dun took his insulin but didn't want no supper."

His physical condition sure fits that of someone in insulin shock.

I kneel down on the dirty floor and feel for a pulse as David opens the trauma kit and takes out the glucometer. I grab his bony wrist. The man is wringing wet and his skin feels like you're touching a big clam.

"Does he have any other medical problems?" David asks the woman.

"He's got some kinda heart trouble but I don't know what it is."

"How old is your dad?" David asks the woman.

"He's 48 and he's my husband," she answers curtly.

I had guessed him to be in his mid-60s. It's obvious David thought the same thing.

David does a finger stick so we can check the patient's blood sugar. He doesn't even react to the needle. David squeezes the man's finger in an effort to milk a drop of blood to put on the test strip. I hold the glucometer next to his finger and we finally get enough when the glucometer starts to count down. It takes a full minute to get a reading. Normal blood sugar is about 100 give or take 20 points either way. If it's below 80 it's considered low. Most people won't go unconscious until it drops below 40 or 50. If it's below 20 it's considered life treating. A patient is considered one step away from death if it's below 10. The meter finally beeps and instead of a number it says LOW. That means his blood sugar is below 10. According to the experts our patient should be dead. If we don't act quickly he might very well be.

Unless they are in very critical shape, which he is, I normally wait until I get the patient into the ambulance before I start IV's and administer medication. This guy can't wait.

"Let's get some D50W in him. I'll look for a vein," I tell David.

I grab a tourniquet out of the kit and loop it around the patient's thin wet upper arm. David digs a bag of saline and IV tubing out of the drug kit and starts getting it ready.

I find one vein in the crook of his arm I think I can get. When you intend to give D50W you have to use a good vein that hopefully won't rupture. D50W stands for 50% dextrose in water. It's literally like shooting several ounces of syrup into your patient's blood stream. If the vein ruptures and the dextrose gets into the surrounding tissue it can cause necrosis.

Diabetics traditionally have very poor and brittle veins. You have to be very careful while starting an IV.

"Let's draw some blood since we didn't get an accurate reading," I tell David.

He grabs a 20 cc syringe, a red, and purple top blood vial from the kit. I stick the needle into the patient's vein and get blood in the flash chamber. I advance the catheter into the vein. David gives me the syringe. I hook it into the catheter and slowly start to draw back on the plunger. I get about 10 cc's and decide not to push my luck. I hand it back to David and he squirts it equally into the two blood vials and then puts the rubber stoppers back. I put the end of the IV tubing into the catheter and release the tourniquet as David opens the valve to start the flow of fluid.

The patient is too diaphoretic to tape down the IV in the traditional way so I use what I call, "you can't pull it out with a truck taping method". You take the one inch cloth tape and go completely around the IV site and the patients arm several times. It doesn't look good but it works. David hands the IV bag to the patient's son and asks him to hold it for us.

I assemble the vial of D50W and stick the needle into the port on the tubing. I slowly start to push on the end of the vial. It takes about a minute to give it all. Usually by the time you give it all the patient starts to wake up. Within the next minute they are fully awake and alert. It is truly a wonderful site to see someone go from unconscious, pale, and shallow breathing to awake and alert within two minutes. I have done it many times but as a doctor I knew once said, "It's like laying on the hands." To think that something as simple as sugar shot into a vein can affect such a change in a patient's condition.

As predicted he starts to moan and groan after about 2 minutes. We have hooked him up to the cardiac monitor and started giving him oxygen during this time. David and I both notice that the T waves are inverted on the cardiac monitor, a possible sign of a heart attack. Since our patient is not conscious we can't determine if he is really having a heart attack since we don't know if he is having chest pain. We have to assume it is a heart attack until proven otherwise.

I figure the patient will be awake in a few minutes and decide to go get the stretcher. I turn to the man's son and ask him to come help me.The boy and I maneuver the stretcher through the waist deep weeds and carefully take it through the front door.

"How's he doing?" I ask David expecting to see our patient awake and able to answer question.

"About the same. He's moaning and groaning but still not answering questions. If I didn't know better I'd swear his blood sugar is still low."

"Let's get him to the ambulance and check it again."

I turn to his wife and tell her what we are going to do.

"Which hospital do you want us to take him to?" I ask her.

"Conroe Medical Center is the closest, I think."

We were so far out in the sticks, close was a relative term. My estimate was that Conroe Medical Center was probably 40 to 50 miles away. The next nearest hospital was probably 50 to 60 miles away in the opposite direction.

"Conroe is fine. That's where we usually take him," she answers.

As David and I lift him onto the stretcher I notice he is still pale as a ghost and wringing wet with sweat.

"Patrick, I think we were right about him having a heart attack," whispers David.

"The thought's crossed my mind," I whisper back. "But we got to get him awake first to see if he's having chest pain."

I turn to his wife and ask if she is going to ride with us to the hospital.

"Yea, we don't have no car. I got to ride with you," she replies.

As we get to the front door, I wonder if we can make it across the porch without falling through. The porch light is on so I look for the nails knowing that is where the joists are. It's not fool proof but if you step where the boards are nailed down you have more support and probably won't fall through. David sees what I'm doing and follows suit. With the patient being light as he is we practically carry him and the stretcher across the porch. A short trip through the jungle and we are at the ambulance. After getting the patient in the unit, David helps his wife into the front seat and comes back to help me get the patient stabilized.

I do another finger stick and the glucometer reads out about the time David gets back.

"What does it say?" he asks.

"Forty, can you believe it even after an amp of D50 it's still only forty."

"Well we knew it was low to start with but it must have been near zero."

We learned later that according to blood we drew initially his blood sugar was only five. Technically he should have been dead. In fact he would have been in a few more minutes if David and I hadn't given him the D50W when we did.

The objective is to get the patient's sugar up to at least 80, so we decide to give him another ampule of dextrose. Since we are so far from the hospital we decide to get started instead of waiting for it to do its magic. The second dose of dextrose does the trick and a few minutes later he wakes up but instead of the usual question "where am I?" He immediately starts clutching his chest and complaining of chest pain. It looks like David and I were right. He finally looks around and realizes he's not at home and that a stranger is taking his blood pressure.

"Who the hell are you?" he asks.

"I'm Patrick. I'm a paramedic and you're in my ambulance. Your wife is up front. Is your chest hurting?"

"It feels like someone's is sitting on it," he grimaces as he says this.

That's usually the way most people describe a heart attack. Some patients are more specific and describe it as an elephant sitting on their chest. His blood pressure is barely high enough to give him medication to relieve the pain. The systolic needs to be over 90 to give morphine or nitro, his is 92 and that's stretching it.

"Ok, I'm going to give you some nitro. Do you normally take that for chest pain?" I ask.

"You mean those little white pills you put under your tongue."

"Yea, except I have the same thing in a spray."

I already had the small aerosol container in hand, "Open your mouth and lift your tongue."

He follows orders and I squirt a metered dose of nitro under his tongue. I look up and see his wife anxiously looking back through the walkway.

"He's awake now," I tell her.

I wait a minute and ask him if the pain is better or worse. He still has the same rhythm on the monitor, sinus rhythm with inverted T waves. The patient tells me it's about the same. According to our protocols, I have to wait five minutes to give him another dose of nitro. By the time I take his blood pressure again it's time for another spray. I see his skin color is still that sickly gray tone that I have seen many, many times with patient's having a heart attack. He also seems to be getting confused a sign that either his sugar level is dropping again or a lack of circulation to his brain due to poor output by his heart. In his case I determine it is probably a combination of both.

I end up giving him two more sprays of nitro, the maximum dose. One of the effects of nitro is to lower blood pressure. That is why it has to be over 90 to start with. By the third dose his pressure has dropped to 80 and he is almost unconscious again. I give him half of an amp of D50W and he wakes up once more. Never before or since did I need to give a patient more than one dose of D50W during transport.

I want to give him morphine for the continuing chest pain but am reluctant to do so because of his low pressure. Not only does morphine relieve the pain, it lessens the amount of oxygen required by the heart muscle and thus helps to minimize damage. His pressure is hanging at the 90 systolic range the bare minimum to be able to give morphine. I decide to call medical control and get permission. I hope that by taking some load off his heart he will quit burning sugar at such alarming rate. I had put 2 and 2 together and assumed the reason for his continued low blood sugar was due to a massive heart attack. I learned later from the doctor that I was right.

Medical control finally gives me permission to give the morphine with the usual lecture of giving it in 2 mg increments until the pain is relieved.

I check with David and find out we are still about 20 minutes away from the hospital. A lot can happen in 20 minutes. As I am unlocking the drug box to get to the morphine I glance at the monitor and see his T waves going even more to the negative and the QRS complex get wider, both signs that the heart attack is getting worse. He is moaning with pain and barely able to answer my questions. I quickly put the prefilled syringe into the holder and lock it in place. I quickly give him the morphine.

I can see the medication take effect by the expression on his face. It goes from a contorted frown to just a frown. I ask him how he feels.

He slowly opens his now glazed eyes and attempts to focus on me and replies, "Pretty good!"

One of the funniest responses I ever got from a patient in that situation.

After what seems like eternity we finally reach the hospital. In reality it did take us almost an hour. In following up, I found out he did indeed have a massive heart attack. Two quick decisions that night, giving more D50W than usual and morphine saved his life. If it had taken just a few more minutes to find him that night he would have died. This call was unusual because the patient had two major medical problems occurring at the same time. Something we rarely saw.

Chapter 9....Total Bone Crunchers

Auto accidents and trauma victims fall into four main categories; minor injuries, major injuries, going to die, and dead. There can be any combination of these at any accident. Triage, french for sort, becomes the responsibility of the first paramedic to arrive at the scene. This is done first thing when you arrive on a scene. You quickly check everyone involved and decide how many patients you have and the severity of their injuries. If you have more than one or two severely injured patients you then have to make several quick decisions. Do you need the rescue squad and or fire department to help extricate the patients that are trapped? How many more ambulances are you going to need? Do you need an air ambulance? If you work in a suburban or metropolitan area you can usually have extra help on the scene in just a few minutes. If you are in a rural area, where most of my experience was, you may have to wait 30 minutes or more to get the extra equipment and assistance you need. In the meantime, you have well-meaning bystanders and sometimes other medical personnel trying to influence your decisions. All things considered, triaging multiple casualty incidents can be the most stressful situation a paramedic will experience. The fear of missing something and having a patient die due to my poor judgment always concerned me. Luckily, I always made the right decisions.

EMS systems have various codes to denote the condition of a patient. In the area I worked the official categories were code 1 meaning minor injuries, code 2 major injuries but not life threading, code 3 life threatening injuries, and code 4 DOA. Over the years we developed our own unofficial codes.

Patients with minor injuries were called "walking wounded." Patients with multiple major injuries were referred to as TBC's short for Total Bone Crunchers. The DOA's were sometimes called DRT "Dead Right There." The most frustrating group were the patients that were going to die. We sometimes referred to them as the "Dead But Don't Know it." These are patients that are alive when you get to them but after assessing their injuries you realize they are probably going to die. Usually they are unconscious but some are not. The patient that is still awake and alert when you make contact but die while you are transporting or shortly after arrival at the hospital were, for me, one of the most difficult situations to handle. You get a feeling of inadequacy. You are doing everything you know to do for them but know it will probably do no good.

When I was a kid my grandmother used to make the statement, "Well, when it's your time to go it's your time to go."

I didn't realize what she meant until I saw people die right in front me in spite of everything we could do for them. The opposite is also true. Patients trapped, crushed, with multiple major fractures that appear to be on the brink of checking out respond to treatment and recover.

My grandmother had a saying for this also, "The good Lord kept them here for some reason."

Famous Last Words

It's spring time and a beautiful sunny Saturday. The Texas blue bonnets are in bloom. Karen and I are going to lunch when we hear the police dispatcher tell her units that an accident has been reported on the access road of the major highway that bypasses town. Karen and I realize we are less than a mile from the location. In fact, we are sitting at the intersection of the access road. I pick up the microphone and ask her if we are going to be needed.

"Yea, it sounds bad. I was just calling your dispatcher. I'll tell them you are responding."

"Yea, show us heading that way."

I hang up the microphone as Karen switches on the lights and siren. I turn left onto the access road. A small hill blocks us from seeing the accident right away but as soon as we top it I see a mattress and a man lying right on the white line of the two lane black-top. Several people are standing around the patient who lies motionless. As I come to a stop I also notice a large puddle of blood under his head.

"He doesn't look too good does he?" I say to Karen as we bail out of the truck.

"Nope, looks pretty much fubared to me."

"Grab the kit. I'll check him out."

The patient is on my side of the ambulance. I get out and immediately see his eyes are wide open and he's not breathing. I quickly scan down his body to check for other injuries. The first thing I see is his lower left arm is missing. Immediately I think, *This is worse than I thought.* He has massive head injuries, he's not breathing, and his arm is amputated. He's dead!

In the next moment I notice his arm was previously amputated. It's an old injury. I feel stupid for not noticing it immediately. I kneel down to check for a pulse not expecting to find one. Before I even touch his neck I can see his carotid artery beating away at about 100 times a minute.

It's obvious he has a massive head injury he can't possible recover from. He's not breathing which means without us breathing for him his heart will stop in a matter of minutes. Even with us assisting his breathing his heart could still stop at any time. He is officially in the "dead but don't know it" category.

During these first few moments I overhear his hysterical wife tell the police office that he had fallen out of the back the pickup. Actually, I found out later, he had been blown off the truck. You see they were moving and had loaded the mattress and box springs onto the bed of the truck crosswise. His wife had asked him if he was going to tie them down.

His last words to her were, "No, since we're only going a couple of miles I'll just sit back here and hold them down. Just don't go too fast."

Witness reported that she was up to about 50 miles an hour when the wind caught the mattress tossing it and the patient approximately 10 feet in the air. He came down head first landing where we found him. Sometimes you make a choice in life and it ends up being a fatal one.

Karen comes around the back of the unit kneels down beside me and whispers, "Is he dead?"

"Nope not yet, his heart's still beating," I say pointing to the pulsing carotid artery.

Karen and I both know the man has a fatal head injury and no matter what we do he will be dead soon. A funny thing happens when you have a call like this, you go into "we're going to save this one" mode. All paramedics I know will do everything within their training and experience treating a patient like this. You know it is useless but somewhere in the back of your mind you hope this patient is the one in a million that will actually make it. Even though you know he won't.

I quickly open the trauma bag and get out the intubation kit. Since he is not breathing this is the first thing we need to take care of before his heart quits. I quickly get the ET tube in place and start to ventilate him.

Jason suddenly shows up and offers to help. He is a fellow paramedic who lives nearby.

"What are you doing here?" Karen asks.

"Sounded bad on the scanner, I thought I would see if y'all need any help."

"What do you think?" Karen replies.

Another thing happens when you are on a serious call such as this. Conversation is held to a minimum, everyone knows what needs to be done. You also move a little faster, like you are racing the angle of death. It becomes a challenge to get the patient to the hospital before he dies. Since the nearest hospital that can handle a patient like this is 20 miles away the race against time is on.

I ventilate the patient while Jason and Karen quickly wrap his head, put on a c-collar and place him on a back board. We lay him on the stretcher and roll him to the back of the ambulance. In less than five minutes after arriving on the scene the patient is in the ambulance. We take vitals, his heart rate is starting to slow down and become irregular.

Karen looks on his good arm for a vein to start an IV in but can't find a suitable one. We make a quick decision and Jason starts the IV his jugular vein.

"OK," I say, "This is a stable as he's going to get, let's boogie. Jason, I need you to ride with me to the hospital."

"But I just stopped to help. I didn't know you would need me to ride. Let me get my truck out of the way and I'll be back in a minute."

That is the way EMS people are. Jason didn't anticipate having to ride the ambulance on his day off but he didn't hesitate to go. He is back in a few seconds and we are ready to go.

"OK Karen let's get there yesterday," I yell through the walk way.

At this point there isn't much more we can do for the patient. We know he is going to die but it is our job to keep him alive as long as possible. I increase the IV drip rate to keep his BP up and continue ventilating him with the bag valve mask. Sure enough about 5 minutes later his heart beat slows and then stops.

We now have a trauma arrest, which is a heart that stops because there is no more blood to pump or the brain is so damaged it no longer sends the signal to the heart to beat. It's difficult enough to get someone back that suffers a cardiac arrest due to medical problems. It is darn near impossible to get a patient back from a trauma arrest.

"Start pumping Jason."

Jason starts chest compressions while I grab the epinephrine out of the drug cabinet. The patient's heart has gone into what is called pulse less electrical activity known as PEA. Which means the electric impulse that makes the heart contract is still present but the heart is no longer contracting.

Using one hand to squeeze the bag mask I hold the epinephrine box in the other. Using my teeth I grab the top and tear it off. I stop ventilating for a few seconds, screw the needle onto the vial and inject the epinephrine into the IV line. Jason continues chest compressions for roughly 20 seconds, about the time it takes for the epinephrine to circulate to the heart.

"Stop compressions," I tell Jason.

I slide my fingers under the c collar to check for a pulse and to my surprise he has regained one.

"He's got a pulse. I can't believe it. He's got a pulse."

Jason and I monitor the patient closely and take turns ventilating him. At any moment we expect his heart to stop again but to our surprise in keeps on beating. In fact the patient lived until the next morning. The family decided to take him off the ventilator.

It is strange how a patient like this becomes a challenge to skills of the paramedics and hospital workers. You assess the patient and in a case like this one you know he is probably not going to live but you do your best to keep him alive.

There are a couple of reasons for this. The main reasons is, especially if the head injury patient is young, is the hope that the patient is an organ donor or that the family can be solicited to donate their organs. The second reason is to do what paramedics are trained to do and that is "get the patient to the hospital alive".

As a paramedic I learned God must look out for people because sometimes they sure don't look out for themselves.

Just Passing By

One beautiful spring morning a 55 year old woman heads outside to do some yard work. She gets into her Lincoln and starts backing out of the car port so she can get to the lawn mower. For reasons unknown she forgets to put the car in park after she stops. It is what I call, "a brain cramp."

She opens the door and puts her left foot on the gravel driveway and starts to get out of the car. At this moment things go downhill quickly and a morning of mowing the lawn turns into months of surgery and rehab. As she does this her right foot comes off the brake and of course the car, still in reverse, starts to roll backwards. Now on a good day most people would have just put their foot back on the brake or picked up their left leg until they got the car stopped. She failed do either one.

Her plan, obviously not well thought out on the spur of the moment, was to leap free of the car. Leaping from any moving vehicle when you are a chubby 55 year old is difficult at best. As she attempts to get footing to make her jump her foot slips and her leg gets caught under the door. She is now being slowly pulled out of the car. Within a few moments she's yanked out and her left foot and lower leg go under the left front tire. She fights to get out of the way, but her body is wedged under the door. During this time her lower leg, now wedged between the tire and the gravel driveway is being ripped to shreds. By the time she is able to wrestle herself from under the door the tire rolls over her already mutilated leg and except for one small muscle it's all but amputated.

This poor lady is now laying in her driveway slowly bleeding to death. No one is home and the nearest neighbor, several hundred yards away, can't hear her calling for help. The road she lives on is fairly well traveled but someone would have to be looking her way to notice. Several cars pass by in the next 20 minutes but no one sees her lying on the driveway waving to attract attention.

This is where God looking out for people comes into play. Two off-duty paramedics from a neighboring EMS service are going to the country to do a little fishing. Keith is the passenger and just happens to be looking the right direction when they pass the lady lying in the driveway. Being both observant and inquisitive, like most paramedics, he tells his partner to turn around so they can see what is wrong.

They pull up into the driveway to find a pale very weak woman lying in a huge puddle of blood, her left leg nearly ripped off below the knee. Robert grabs the first aid kit that practically all paramedics carry in their cars, and quickly bandages her legs.

We head towards the call but the patient lives out in the country and it will take us at least 20 minutes to get there. As luck would have it, and believe me this patient needs it, one of our first responders who lives in the area is just a few minutes away and quickly arrives on the scene.

Kathy radios us after only being on the scene a couple of minutes and quickly lets us know about the amputation and suggests that we call for Lifeflight. Thinking ahead, Kathy knows the only hope the patient has of possibly having her leg reattached is at Herman hospital the closest level one trauma center. Since Herman is about 90 miles away transporting her there by air ambulance will get her there much quicker than we can. I radio our dispatcher tell her to get Lifeflight heading to the scene.

I turn into the gate and pull up to where everyone's gathered. I recognize Robert but am surprised to see him since Kathy did not mention the other medics being on the scene.

"Aren't you a little north of your usual territory?" I ask sarcastically.

"Heard you' all weren't able to handle it so we thought we would come bail you out." was Roberts quick comeback.

As we package the patient for transport Kathy and Robert fill me in on what happened to the patient.

The Sheriff's deputy tells me that they are going to land the helicopter in the cow pasture across the road and that they are 10 minutes away. We place the patient in the ambulance for the short ride across the street.

The patient had an injury where time was of great importance if the leg was to be saved. On this particular day many things came together in her favor. Two off duty paramedics come along within a few minutes of the accident and just happen to notice her and stop. Kathy was on the ball and quickly assessed the situation and made the decision to call for the helicopter instead of waiting for us to get there.

Life flight was available and was on the scene quickly and because we already had the patient packaged was able to load her and be back in the air with in a few minutes. Surgeons at the hospital were able to take the mutilated remains of her lower leg and reattach them saving her from amputation. The patient recovered and was up and walking on the leg within a few months.

Breakfast of Champions

Early one morning we receive a call for a major accident at a busy intersection where accidents were quite common. An elementary school is located about a block off the main road. There is no traffic light so after dropping their children off parents have to jump onto the main road into busy morning traffic. Most accidents at this intersection are minor because a lot of people who live in the area slow down when they are near. That was not the case on this particular morning.

As usual I start to assess the scene as we approach. I see one patient lying in the middle of the street with several people around her. I also see a red Camaro smashed into a telephone pole with Bill, a first responder, attending to someone in the driver's seat of that vehicle.

"Go help Bill. I'll check out the one in the street," I tell Shirley as we come to a stop.

I approach the woman lying in the street. I notice several wrecker drivers standing around and another woman kneeling, holding her head.

"I'm the school nurse. I heard the wreck happen and ran down to help. She's got a really bad open fracture of her left lower leg."

With that said, the nurse throws back the coat that is covering the patient's legs. To put it mildly, I am surprised at what I see. The fracture the nurse referred to is in reality a severely crushed lower leg. The calf of the patient's left leg is virtually flat. Bone, muscle, skin, and fat combine to look like hamburger. The odd thing is, no bleeding. In a crushing injury such as this there is very little if any bleeding due to blood vessels that were crushed being closing off.

Suddenly I see movement out of the corner of my eye. I look up just in time to see a large man wearing a dirty T-shirt, hit the pavement. Lucky for him his fellow wrecker driver's catch him, more or less, as he faints in a heap in the middle of the street.

The school nurse was obviously trying not alarm the patient by describing the injury as an open fracture instead of what it was, a near amputation. As I am assessing the patient's overall condition, the wrecker drivers are attempting to wake up Bubba. They start asking me to do something for him.

I lean over and whisper to them, "Listen, I have someone really hurt here, I don't have time to mess with a big tough wrecker driver who fainted. Just leave him alone. He'll wake up in a few minutes."

This statement upsets his buddies, but it was the truth.

"I'll be back in a minute. I need to go get some equipment," I tell the nurse.

As I head to the ambulance, Shirley comes running up to me.

"We need help with the other patient," she says.

I look over to see he is on the stretcher and they have already loaded him into the ambulance.

"What's wrong?" I ask.

"He's not breathing and we don't think he has a pulse," she tells me in an excited voice.

"You don't think he has a pulse. What do you mean you don't think he has a pulse? Either he has one or he doesn't," I say sternly.

"Well we can't feel one. We want to see what you think," she says as we head for the ambulance.

"When did he loose a pulse?" I ask.

I assumed that the loss of pulse had been only a few moments ago.

"He never had one," she says.

"He never had one. What do you mean he never had one?" I ask as I get into the ambulance.

To make matters even worse I find the patient lying face down on the backboard. A backboard does no good if it the patient's not lying on his back. It's now getting difficult not to get upset with my partner and the first responder. Since I can't tell what type of injuries he has or for that matter anything about the patient I roll him over onto his back. To my surprise he's looking back at me. Not that he could see me, because he was in fact without question dead. Eyes wide open and bugged out, face purple, tongue swollen, and neck veins protruding, a condition known as Traumatic Asphyxia. It's the result of a severe crushing injury to the chest, in this case, hitting the steering wheel. This was back before cars had air bags. With this type of injury the heart is crushed along with lungs. Blood is forced into the head of the patient causing everything from the neck up to swell and turn purple. It was obvious he hadn't been wearing a seatbelt; if he had he probably would have walked away. Bill and Shirley are right about two things he's not breathing and he has no pulse. Even though he's a young man in his mid 20s there is nothing we can do for him.

I had made a mistake when I first arrived on the scene of trusting someone that I knew was prone to get excited and not always think things thought. Bill appeared to be tending to the patient in the car and never once said anything about the patient being dead. In Shirley's defense she was very new to EMS at that time and had only made a few calls. Knowing Bill had more experience she followed his lead, which is a natural thing to do in this type of situation. In retrospect I should have checked him before checking on the condition of the woman lying in the street.

I don't have time to figure out why they loaded a dead man in my ambulance. I need to get back to my patient with the crushed leg. I turn to Shirley and Bill who are standing outside the back door of the unit waiting for me to start CPR or something when I tell them in no uncertain terms.

"Get this dead man out of my ambulance!"

"Do what?" Bill asks confused.

Trying to maintain control of a bad situation that's getting worse, I tell them, "There nothing I can do for him, get him out of my ambulance so I can take care of the other patient."

I start to collect the equipment I need to bandage and splint the other patients crushed leg. I grab what I need and head back to the woman lying in the street.

Even though Bill knows I am very upset he still manages to say something stupid.

"Where are we going to put the body?"

"I don't care, just get him out," I say in as stern a voice as I can.

I get back to the other patient and the nurse and I begin to bandage and splint the leg. I notice that the foot has no circulation in it. *Not a good sign,* I think. As we package the patient I realize I don't know who hit who or anything about the accident itself. The patient is conscious so I ask her what happened.

"I just dropped my kid off at school and was trying to get out. I guess I didn't see that red car and pulled out in front of it. I was thrown out of my truck and it ran over my leg."

I now know how her leg got crushed. Of course if she had also been wearing her seat belt she wouldn't have lost her leg. Yes, she did lose the leg.

Shirley shows up with the stretcher and helps me finish packaging the patient.

"We put him in the rescue truck," she tells me as we roll the patient to the ambulance.

I am doing what is called a secondary survey to see if the patient has any other injuries I may have missed when a sheriff's deputy sticks his head in the door and asks to see the patient's driver's license. She tells him it's in her purse which is still in the truck. He goes to get the purse just as the local Justice of the Peace arrives on the scene.

In Texas, judges have the authority to pronounce someone dead. It goes back to the cowboy days. Back then when someone died, the nearest doctor might be days away. So the state of Texas gave that authority to the local judges. In most rural counties in Texas this is still the way it is done. Only in the bigger cities do they have Medical Examiners.

The judge's office was nearby, so she was able to get there before we left the scene. It was lucky for me that I was on first name basis with her.

She opens the door and asks, "Why did you take the body out of the car and put it the back of the rescue truck?"

It's a big no, no to move a dead body until the Judge says so.

"I didn't put him anywhere," I replied.

"Then who did?"

I move closer to the door and whisper to her a short version of what happened.

"Ok, I just wanted to know," she says.

About then the deputy returns with the purse. It is one of those large bag type purses.

"Mam, can I get your license out of here or do you want to do it?" he asks.

You can get it," she says.

The officer opens the purse and reaches in to get her wallet but abruptly stops. He motions me to look in the purse. In the bottom of it are 4 cans of cold beer.

Well, I think, *That explains why I thought I smelled beer on her breath.*

I had convinced myself I was wrong due to it being 8 o'clock in the morning and the fact that she was driving her kid to school.

I have always said that about the time I think I have seen everything I see something else. This is one of those cases. Being addicted to alcohol is tragic. In this case she killed someone and lost her leg, not to mention disrupting and destroying the dead man's family and her own.

To this day I wonder how she managed to fall out of her own vehicle in such a way that only her leg was run over. The damage to her truck was minimal. The man died from the secondary impact; that is, hitting the telephone pole after hitting her. I think that in the panic of the moment she jumped from her truck. Why? Who knows? People do some pretty dumb things when they are drunk. On the other hand, they also do dumb things where they aren't.

The Tractor and the Nut

The man who ran over himself with his tractor hadn't been drinking. He did what all of us have done at one time or another. He just didn't think for a few seconds. In this case it cost him his life.

Picture this. You own a tree farm. You are very busy so busy in fact you just never got around to tightening that 9/16 nut that holds the battery cable to the starter solenoid on your tractor. Instead you stand next to the engine and wiggle the cable while you push the start button on the dash. This works until the day you forget to put the tractor in neutral before wiggling the cable. On that day the tractor starts, lurches forward, and you are knocked down and run over by the one of its large tires. Got the picture? That's good because it happened one morning to a very nice elderly gentleman.

Jason and I arrive on the scene and see the patient lying on his back between rows of trees. At first glance he didn't appear to be that badly injured but as the saying goes, "looks can be deceiving."

He is still conscious and wants to get up and go back to work.

"Where do you hurt?" is usually the first question I ask a conscious trauma patient.

As they answer or at least attempt to, I do what we call a primary survey. It is a quick head to toe check for any outward signs of injury. I look for things such as profuse bleeding and apparent fractures. Anything that could immediately threaten the patient's life we stop and treat. Sometimes the injuries are apparent. Sometimes they are not.

"Oh I'll be ok. Just let me lie here and rest a minute," he tells us as we kneel down by him.

"What happened?" Jason asked.

"I've been meanin' to tighten that nut for a while now," he says.

"What nut?" I ask.

"On the damn tractor! The nut on the solenoid, I meant to tighten it," he says angrily and then he starts to drift off a little.

After a moment of mumbling to himself, he continues insisting he's OK and to let him get up.

"Just let me go back to work," he tells us.

About that time a worker at the farm, who witnessed the whole thing, steps up and tells us he saw the big rear wheel of the tractor run over his legs.

"Where do you hurt?" asked Jason since we didn't get an answer the first time we asked.

"My leg hurts a little. Just let me rest a minute and I'll be OK," he repeats.

Jason and I exchange glances. It's starting to look like this man is hurt pretty bad. He's wearing overalls that make it difficult to see anything. Using our paramedic scissors we cut the legs of his overalls up to the waist. As we expose his left leg we see tire marks running from just above his ankle all the way up to his waist. The muscles in his thigh are knotted and bunched up. When his upper body moves, his leg doesn't. All obvious signs of a broken femur.

Due to what we call "implement of injury" Jason and I determine that his left femur and hip are probably crushed. This is a very serious injury especially for older patients. The immediate problem with a broken hip and femur is the probability of internal bleeding. In this instance, we not only have the possibility of bleeding from the fractures, we also have the good chance he is bleeding from other internal injuries to his abdomen.

"Sir, we're paramedics. You're hurt and we need to take you to the hospital," Jason informs him.

"Hurt, I ain't hurt. Who called y'all? All I need to do is to fix that damn tractor. Let me up so I can get back to work."

It was odd he kept telling us to let me up when no one was or had been holding him down. Even though he told us to let him up, he makes no attempt to do so. In the few minutes since making contact with him, he has become confused. The patient's confusion along with pale skin all add up to a patient going into shock.

We are only 15 minutes from a hospital that can handle this type of injury, so we decide to do what is called load and go. Basically you package the patient as quickly as you can and haul butt to the hospital. Even with all of the advance stuff paramedics can do, we still can't stop internal bleeding. The best treatment is quick transport so the patient can get to surgery.

By the time we package him and head for the hospital, which probably takes us about five or six minutes, more signs of shock from internal bleeding are staring to develop. His blood pressure is dropping, his heart rate is increasing, and he is becoming more and more confused.

I get an IV on him while we are going down the highway and start to infuse it at a rapid rate. While saline solution does not replace blood, it does replace the liquid part that is lost and helps to maintain the patient's blood pressure for a little while.

As we pull into the emergency entrance of the hospital, he has become somewhat more alert and I begin to think he might have a chance. Unfortunately he died three days later.

This man was well known and liked by many people in the local community. If he had just tightened that "damn nut" as he put it, he would probably have lived a good while longer.

Stand Aside I'm a Doctor

A lot of modern motorcycle "gangs" consist of doctors, lawyers and various other professionals running around on $20,000 Harley's on weekends. It's a beautiful late autumn day on a Sunday afternoon when just such a gang decided to take a ride in the county. Fall is one of the prettiest times of the year in South East Texas. On this day it's about 80 degrees and not a cloud in the sky, a perfect day for a motorcycle ride.

The call comes in from dispatch to respond to an MVA, short for motor vehicle accident. No details are given other than location but it is on a particularly crooked stretch of two lane road where accidents happen quite often.

Karen and I have been in route to the call for several minutes and are starting to wonder if the dispatcher has any more information. Usually they give the ambulance minimal information initially and call us back a few minutes later and give details.

"Medic 7 to dispatch."

"Dispatch, go ahead," she replies.

"Do you have any more details on the call?" I ask.

"Medic 7, the call came in on a cell phone. The connection was bad. All I could get was the location and they needed an ambulance. Unit 642 is on his way. He's close and should be there soon."

"Well, that's the exciting part of EMS," jokes Karen. "You never know what you're getting into. Guess we'll wait and see what the deputy says once he gets there."

Sure enough the deputy arrives on the scene a few minutes later. In less than a minute he radios us.

"642 to Medic 7."

Good, we think, he is going to let us know what is going on.

"Medic 7 go ahead," I respond.

"Medic 7, uh, there are people here telling me to call for Lifeflight. Do you want me to do that?" he asks hesitantly.

Karen and I look at each other wondering if one of our first responders might be on the scene without their radio. Still it was odd, usually the deputy would have told us that a first responder was requesting Lifeflight or they would have come on the radio and talked to us directly.

"642, who is requesting Lifeflight?" I ask.

There are several moments of silence before he comes back on the radio. "Medic 7 there's a doctor here that says he needs Lifeflight right now."

"That's just great," says Karen. "All we need is doctor on the scene trying to order us around."

I agree with her. Over the years as ambulances have become more advanced in their ability to care for a patient, sometimes this becomes a problem when a doctor is on the scene.

They mean well but it normally causes a conflict. Paramedics follow a set of rules for treating patients. They are called protocols. Protocols are written orders that the medical director, a doctor, of the EMS service signs off on that give paramedics the authority to start IVs and give medication to patients without having to call a doctor every time. In most cases these written orders follow a standard of care established by several different organizations. They are modified for each service but most are very similar.

Doctors not familiar with and not trained in Advance Cardiac Life Support and Advance Trauma Life Support sometimes want to do treatment that is contrary to what paramedics are permitted to perform. It's a problem that comes up at times on all ambulances. Most have found that if a doctor insists on telling us how to treat a patient, we tell him he's responsible for the patient and will have to ride to the hospital with them. This statement usually gets the doctor off our back so we can do our job. On a couple of occasions an actual ER doctor stops to help which usually works out because they understand how paramedics operate. We can only hope that this is the case but know it probably isn't.

By this time we are only about 10 minutes from the scene of the accident so we tell the deputy to wait until we get there. A few minutes later he calls us again.

"642 to Medic 7, the doctor says to hurry up."

Being told to "hurry up" over the radio bothers me worse that just about anything else you can tell me. It is said quite often to us as we heading to a call. I realize that time slows down for the people at the scene but being told to hurry up implies, to me anyway, that we are just cruising along taking our time to get to the call. I have even had patients and their family members imply I took my time getting to a call because they were a minority. This is ridiculous; dispatchers don't have time along with everything else going on to tell us, "Oh, by the way these people are a minority so take your time."

We round the corner and the scene comes into view. There are about 15 Harley's parked all over the road and one lying in the ditch along with the patient. Karen and I see two people doing CPR on him.

The deputy called us several times to request Lifeflight and to tell us to hurry up but couldn't find the time to tell us it was a motorcycle accident and CPR was in progress. Guess he didn't think it was important.

"Grab everything," I tell Karen as we come to a stop.

I jump out and grab the advance kit while she gets the basic kit and the cardiac monitor/defibrillator.

As I kneel down by the patient the person doing CPR starts talking. "I'm a doctor we need to get this man intubated now."

"Well no kidding," I think, as I throw open the intubation kit and quickly get out the laryngoscope and an endotracheal tube.

The patient is cyanotic and not breathing but has no obvious external injuries.

"What happened?" I ask.

I was curious to find out if there had really been an accident or if the patient had a medical problem. The woman helping to do CPR, we later learned was the doctor's wife and a nurse herself, speaks up.

"He lost control of the bike on the curve and flew over the handle bars."

"He flew about 20 feet landing on his head. When I got to him he mouthed the words I can't breathe, then went out, I think he broke his neck," blurts out the doctor.

"Ok, I'm ready to intubate," I tell him.

"I'll do it," the doctor tells me reaching for the equipment.

"No offenses but what kind of doctor are you?" I ask.

"I'm an anesthesiologist at Methodist," he says curtly.

I hand him the scope and tube. There is very good chance he has intubated many more people than I have or ever will. What he hasn't done is intubate them lying in a ditch, I have. He tries a couple of times and then says he can't see the vocal cords.

"Let's just get him in the ambulance and I'll intubate him there," he says frustrated.

"Let me give it a shot," I say.

I lie down on the ground and get the tube into the trachea within a few seconds. The one thing I have always been good at is intubations. It even seemed to impress the doctor. During this time Karen discovers the patient has regained a heartbeat. After ventilating the patient with oxygen for a few minutes his color returns.

We start to package the patient by putting a c-collar on him and placing him on a backboard. Karen and I do this along with the help of the doctor and his wife.

"Are you going to call for Lifeflight?" the doctor asks again.

"We are only about 20 minutes from the hospital and it will take the helicopter over 45 minutes to get here," I tell him. He understands.

After packaging the patient, he is placed on the stretcher, rolled carefully to the ambulance, and lifted in. All this time the patient has been totally unconscious and in full arrest for a period of several minutes. I was at the head ventilating him with the bag valve mask, a device that forces oxygen into the lungs.

As we lock the stretcher into place, I sit down on what is called the captain's chair. It is located at the head of the stretcher. During the process of rolling the patient into the ambulance, I was concentrating on walking backwards while squeezing the BVM every 5 seconds. After sitting down, I look at the patient's face and to my great surprise he's looking back at me. To get someone back from a full cardiac arrest is a very rare event. It is almost unheard of to get someone back from a trauma arrest. I am not sure if he is aware of what is going on or not although his eyes seem to be following me.

When someone is intubated they are unable to talk. The tube that goes into the trachea goes past your vocal cords. Since no air is passing over them you can't talk. Of course when someone who has been intubated wakes up the first thing they try to do is talk. This patient is no exception. I can see the frightened look in his eyes as he tries to make sense of what he sees and hears. His lips start to move but of course no sound comes out.

"Sir, I'm a paramedic and you are in an ambulance. You had a wreck on your motorcycle. You have a tube in your lungs that is helping you breathe so you won't be able to talk for a while. If you understand me blink once," I tell him. He blinks once.

"Is he really awake?" asked the doctor. He is as astonished as I am.

"Yes he is," I answer.

So that the patient can see him, the doctor comes to the head of the stretcher and tries to reassure him and explain what is happening. He also tells the patient he will meet him at the hospital. The patient seems to understand as his friend leaves the ambulance.

Karen has gotten an IV during this time and we are ready to head to the hospital. Karen and I notice that the patient's arms and legs haven't moved and that he didn't seem to feel the stick from the IV needle. It's starting to look as if the good doctor is right about the patient breaking his neck. I deduct that the break must be high as C1 or C2 since he is making no attempt to breathe on his own.

There are 7 cervical vertebras. If a person breaks his neck at the lower part say at C5 or C6 usually they can still breathe on their own. Their legs will be paralyzed and they will probably have very little use of their arms. If a person breaks his neck higher up it impairs his diaphragm muscles and they will either have great difficulty breathing or not be able to breathe at all. These patients will need to be on a respirator.

We have been heading to the hospital for about 10 minutes when the patient appears to become aware of the fact he can't move or feel anything. Up to this point he has been fairly calm. All of a sudden he starts chewing on the ET tube and trying to talk. It doesn't matter how many times I tell him he can't talk, he keeps trying. Then when I can't understand him he becomes even more agitated. I realize he wants to know what happened and the extent of his injuries and I do my best to tell him. It seems that no matter what I say to him it's not the information he wants. It doesn't take him long to get very worked up. My efforts to reassure him only seem to make matters worse.

I get Karen's attention through the walk way, "Call Med Com and see if I can him give some Valium or Versed, he's getting pretty upset."

Med Com was our abbreviation for Medical Control. Karen picks up the cell phone and makes the call. They are already aware of the patient and his condition and they have called the hospital to let them know we are coming.

After a minute or so Karen hangs up the cell phone, "They said go ahead and give him 5 milligrams of Valium to start and 5 more if the first dose doesn't do the trick."

Ten milligrams of valium is usually considered a pretty good dose. The reason you give it in increments is so the patient doesn't stop breathing. In this case it doesn't matter.

Now that I have permission, how am I going to get it out of the lock box on the other side of the ambulance? Having to ventilate the patient every 5 seconds or so makes it a bit difficult. I tell the patient that I am going to get up for a few seconds to get something. I hope that by telling him what is going to happen it will not upset him anymore than he already is.

Even though it is ideal to ventilate every 5 seconds or so you can go a little longer if you have to. I give him a count down and jump up with the keys and head for the back. Getting the key in to the lock while we are traveling down the road at 80 mph takes a few seconds longer that I anticipate. Of course being in a hurry doesn't help. I finally get it unlocked grab the small plastic box that contains morphine, Valium, and Versed and make my way back to the head of the stretcher.

The patient is still trying to ask questions and as I expected getting more upset every second. I quickly grasp the BVM and start to ventilate him again.

At one time we carried the narcotics in prefilled syringes. You just twisted the needle to lock it and you were ready. Months earlier in a cost saving measure the prefills had been replaced with vials. These vials are all glass. The top has to be broken off and the needle stuck into the vial so you can suck up the medication.

With one hand bagging the patient I get as prepared as I can. I tear open the package containing the syringe and alcohol prep using my teeth. I then line everything up in order. I tell the patient that I am going to stop ventilating him again and give him the old 5 count. As fast as I can, I grab the gauzes and placed it over the top of the vial so I can break it without cutting my thumb. The one time I didn't do this little safety exercise I, you guessed it, cut my thumb. I pick up the syringe, put the needle cover in my mouth and pulled it out. I then draw up the medication. The juggling act over, I grab the BVM and quickly give the patient several deep breaths. The whole process probably takes less about 15 seconds.

I know that as agitated as he is and as big as he is that 5 mg probably will not faze him. I am tempted to go ahead and give all ten mgs at once but so I can say that I followed orders I give him the first five wait about a minute and give the rest. It helps some but he is still understandably very confused and agitated. I have done everything I can do for him. I continue talking to him and trying to figure out what he is attempting to say. It's frustrating for him and me.

We arrive at the emergency room in less than 20 minutes and quickly tell the doctor and nurses what happened. They are as amazed as we were that he had regained consciousness.

The doctor orders x-rays of his neck to see where and how badly it's broken. When the tech comes back in a few minutes with the films I am as anxious at the doctor is to see them. The ER doctor slides them into the viewer and turns on the light. It doesn't take an x-ray tech or a doctor to see that his first and second cervical vertebras are completely shattered.

According to the doctor the chances of surviving his injuries are practically nonexistent especially since the patient is 67 years old. With a spinal injury that high up, quite often the internal organs begin to fail one by one. His prognosis is not good.

In a situation like this you wonder why he was revived only to die two weeks later. It brings meaning to the old saying. "It just wasn't his time." In the long run you learn not worry about why for very long. It can drive a paramedic crazy if you try to figure out why some patients die and some live when you think they shouldn't have. You do your best and leave it in God's hands.

Picking a Fight you Can't Win

It's dusk when Sharla and I are dispatched to an auto/train wreck at an intersection near downtown. We arrive quickly to find an old Buick with moderate right front damage in the ditch next to the crossing. A woman and two teenage girls are walking around outside the car. The train has come to a stop and is blocking the intersection. At first glance no one appears to be hurt.

"Looks like they may have lucked out," I say prematurely to Sharla.

We get out and ask if anyone is hurt.

"My son's in the car. I can't wake him up," the woman tells us, as Sharla and I start toward the car.

I go around to the other side of the car that we can't see from where we parked. To my surprise, I see a blond head sticking out of the broken right rear window of the car. He is face down and hanging by his neck on the bottom of the window frame. It's difficult to see his face until I get right up to him. He's pale, obviously unconscious, and not breathing. Because of the angle he's hanging I can't get to his neck to feel for a pulse.

'Can you feel anything?" ask Sharla.

"No I can't. See if you can get to him from inside," I tell her.

In a moment, she's maneuvered her way into the back seat and up next to the patient. She lifts him up just enough to get her

240

fingers in position to feel for a carotid pulse. As soon as she does, he takes a deep breath and starts to breathe. Sharla confirms a pulse.

"Hold him there. I'll get the stretcher," I tell her as I head for the ambulance.

I return quickly and wriggle myself into the back seat. Sharla continues to hold his airway open while I make a very quick check to see if the he has any other obvious injuries. He doesn't appear to have any but in this case it really doesn't matter. Since it's clear he's probably suffered a severe head injury, we've made the decision to do what is called a rapid extrication. That's where you get the patient out and to the ambulance as quickly as possible. Normally with a patient that has been in an accident you take extra time to immobilize their neck and back before moving them. This is done to keep from making any possible neck or back injury they may have worse. In the case of a life threatening injury, such as this, you get the patient out as quickly as possible while attempting to minimize movement of the neck and spine. Like many things, what you are supposed to do and what you end up doing in real life are two different things. In this case the patient was in the back seat of a two door car. He probably weighed around 140 pounds and was unconscious.

If you haven't had the experience of attempting to move an unconscious person, think of it as trying to maneuver 140 pounds of bread dough. You just can't get a hold of it and just when you think you have, it slips away. Now try to imagine getting that same 140 pounds of dough out of the back of a two door car. If you can imagine that, you have rough idea of Sharla and me getting this patient out of the car and on to the stretcher. In paramedic school they teach you how to treat almost every life threatening emergency. You even practice them but we never practiced getting an unconscious patient out of the back seat of a two door car. It's one of those on the job learning experiences.

We finally succeed in sliding him on to the backboard and securing a C collar. In less than five minutes from the time we arrived, he is in the ambulance. Sharla is getting a set of vitals before we roll, while I do a secondary exam. It doesn't look good; I can already see the signs of a severe head injury starting to develop. He has developed what is called "coons eyes" which refers both eyes being blackened like that of a raccoon. He also has "battle signs" which is swelling and discoloration behind the ears. These signs along with being unconscious and flying headlong going through a car window, all point to severe bleeding of the brain and surrounding tissue. It's called a closed head injury. The coon's eyes and battle signs showing up this quickly after the accident indicate he is already in critical condition.

This was a difficult call with several unanswered or unexplained questions. First and foremost, why didn't his mother stop for the train. Since the train was going through town it was only going about 30 mph. Also, the crossing lights and bells were working. Second, why was everyone else wearing a seat belt? In the 10 minutes or so I was on the scene, the mother never answered these two questions.

In the end, it really didn't matter. His mother will have to live with the fact that either due to not watching what she was doing or thinking she could "beat the train" her son died.

Round Two with a Train

Many years later in Grimes County, Texas I was dispatched to another heart breaking auto-train accident. This time at an intersection far out in the country that was only marked with signs. Like the previous story it is dusk.

Karen and I arrive on the scene only being told that a car had been hit by a train. The first thing I notice is a small compact car that, like the Buick, in the previous story didn't seem to be that badly damaged.

The first patient I see is a middle aged woman in a red dress sitting up next to the car with one of our first responders taking care of her. She doesn't appear too badly hurt. The next patient I spot is a heavy set man lying next to the tree line which is about 50 or 60 feet from the point of impact. He is conscious and several people are kneeling down beside him. I would soon find out he had been thrown that distance. Just past the man about 10 feet into the trees I see two bodies lying about 20 feet apart. This puts them about 70 feet from the point of impact. I don't know if anyone else has seem them or not but no one is taking care of them. I can also see that neither one of them is moving.

In the meantime Karen has also done a quick check of the scene.

"Ok Karen, I see 4 patients. Do you see any more?" I ask.

"I don't see any more, but you know how it is," she says.

"Yep, I do," I reply.

We know that in an auto accident patients can be thrown, crawl, or dragged a long way from the vehicle they were riding in. You learn to look in ditches, trees, ponds or anywhere a body might land. You may wonder why we just don't ask other people involved in the accident how many people were with them. We do but depending on how serious the accident is and how confused the other patients are you might get a variety of answers.

At one call firefighters and bystanders combed a fairly large area for about fifteen minutes looking for a baby that the mother insisted had been in the car with her. We found an empty child safety seat in the car but no child. It was night and we had visions of the baby ending up almost anywhere. Finally after getting the hysterical mother to calm down a little bit she tells us her baby might not have been in the car after all and she might be with her grandmother. After getting her to remember her mother's phone number we call her and are relieved to hear that the baby is with her.

We both take a quick look at the surrounding area but can't spot any more patients.

"You check the man and the woman," I said, pointing to the woman sitting by the car and the man by the trees. "I'll check these two," indicating the ones in the woods.

As I make my way towards the closest patient I can see it's a girl who appears to be about 12 years old. She's not breathing and her body is badly contorted. I check for a pulse knowing she doesn't have one. I quickly determine she cannot be helped due to the massive multiple injuries she has sustained. I make my way to the other patient, also a young lady that appears to be about the same age, to find she has suffered a similar death. I look up and see several small trees bent over and broken, evidence of path they took as they flew the estimated 70 feet so from the car.

Making the decision to attempt resuscitation of a trauma arrest is based on several factors. On a trauma call such as this, you have to make an educated guess as to what injuries the patient has sustained. Then you determine if these injuries are or aren't incompatible with life. This means you determine that even if you could get this patient's heart started again would they be able to live. In a nutshell, what you do is make an educated guess as to why their heart quit. Did they bleed to death either internally or externally? Since we don't carry blood on ambulances even if you could get enough fluid into the cardiovascular system to get the heart to beat it doesn't carry oxygen. The major organs like brain and heart die within 5 minutes without it. Is their nervous system intact? Do they still have the majority of their brain and is it connected to the rest of their body? Did a bullet go through their heart and destroy it, likewise for the brain. These and many more are considered injuries incompatible with life.

Since these girls obviously have several injuries that are indeed incompatible with life, I make the decision there is nothing that can be done for them.

Karen has assessed the other patients by now and I go to where she is attending to the man.

"What have you got?" I ask.

Karen stands up and walks a few feet away from him with me following. "He was thrown from the car and landed where he is now. And of course he wasn't wearing his seat belt. He's hurt pretty bad. I think he may have some internal bleeding going on. I can't see any fractures but he's guarding his belly. He's conscious but a little confused. I think we should fly him," Karen tells me.

"How about the woman?"

"She doesn't seem to be hurt from what I can see. She's the only one that was wearing a seat belt. How about your two?" Karen asks.

"They're gone," I tell her.

"You know one of them is their daughter don't you?"

"I didn't know for sure but I figured as much. I wonder who the other one is."

I tell Karen to start packaging the patients as I head for the ambulance to call for Lifeflight and another ambulance for the mother. Karen enlists the help of several first responders that have now shown up on the scene.

I am quickly informed by dispatch that Lifeflight is not available due to bad weather in Houston. I am upset by this information. Lifeflight could have gotten the man to the hospital in less than an hour, the golden hour as it is called in emergency medicine. Studies have shown that if a trauma patient can get to a hospital and definitive care within an hour their chances of survival are greatly improved.

The nearest hospital is about 20 miles away but it is a small county hospital that's not capable of handling his injuries. The nearest hospital that can handle him is about 40 miles away. We have no choice but to get him in the ambulance and transport as quickly as possible.

I hang up the microphone and go check on mom and dad. I get to the mother first. While she doesn't appear to have any severe injuries, she's dazed and somewhat confused. She's asking about her daughter and her friend. The first responders have found out that the other girl was a neighbor and good friend of their daughter. They had invited her to go out to dinner with them.

Unless a patient knows for sure that someone else involved in the accident is dead I never tell them. I have always thought they should be told in a more controlled environment. I don't lie to them or give them false hope I just don't tell them everything. My standard answer is to tell them the other person is very serious and that everything is being done for them. It's just kind of an unwritten rule that most paramedics I know follow.

I know in the movies and on TV it shows the paramedics telling the patient they aren't going to make it. I guess this is so they can take care of unfinished business or something like that before they die. I can't think of anything worse than telling a critical patient they are probably going to die and causing them to give up hope.

I then go over to where the first responders, Kathy and Don are helping Karen immobilize the father. He is conscious for now but due to the fact he was thrown 50 feet or so and weighs about 300 pounds we are almost certain he has internal injuries. He's complaining of pain in his abdomen and difficulty breathing, both signs of possible internal bleeding. After I reassess him I see that Karen is right, he is hurt badly.

"Lifeflight's not available, so we need to get going. I have the other unit coming for his wife," I tell them.

I go back to check on the mother and to make sure she has remained stable. After talking with the first responders and her, I see she's unchanged. In a multiple patient situation the first paramedic on the scene has the responsibility of assessing and reassessing all of the patients involved.

The father has now been loaded into my ambulance. Karen goes to look after the mother until the other unit arrives while Kathy and Don, the first responders, help me with the father. I quickly reassess him and see he is having more difficulty breathing than just a few moments before. I listen to his breath sounds to see if he possibly has a collapsed of partially collapsed lung. The breath sounds are equal but a little diminished. Many times patients who are hurting breathe shallower in an attempt to keep from hurting. It makes it difficult to determine if they actually have a respiratory problem or not. I check his abdomen and find it's even more tender than it was the last time I checked. He's getting worse by the moment.

"We need to go now!" I tell Kathy, "Get on the radio and see how far away the other ambulance is. If they are more than a few minutes away I am going to leave Karen here and you and Don will go with me to the hospital."

Since Karen and I are the only paramedics on the scene we cannot leave the other patient with lesser trained medical personnel. Even though she's not hurt bad it's called abandonment, which is a big no no.

If necessary I am going to let one of the first responders drive the ambulance for me. While they are allowed to ride in the back and help us attend to the patient it's against company policy to let someone who isn't an employee drive one of our units. I wouldn't be the first time I have done this. It's always easier to be forgiven than to get permission.

I hear on the radio that the other unit is just moments away; in fact I can hear their siren.

"Kathy you are going to ride with me and help. Don, as soon the other unit pulls up, show them the other patient and get Karen in here so we can go."

"Kathy, get an IV setup!"

Just as she opens the cabinet the other ambulance pulls up. Don jumps out to do as I asked and in a flash Karen is back and jumps into the driver's seat.

"Y'all ready back there?" she asks.

"Yep, let's boogey."

We head for the hospital having only been on the scene for about 12 minutes. Not too bad.

Kathy has the IV ready and I start it "on the roll" as it is called by paramedics. That's when an IV is started while moving down the road. People have often asked me how you start an IV on someone in the back of a bumpy ambulance.

My pat answer has always been to say, "Well you get the IV needle as close as you can to the vein you intend to stick and wait for the next big bump to knock into place." While this simplified answer often gets me a laugh it's not far from the truth.

We are still about 30 minutes from the hospital when I notice the patient's mental status starting to deteriorate. He's becoming confused and wanting to go to sleep. He was fully conscious when we first made contact with him. Now his skin is pale and cool, his breathing more labored, and his heart rate's increasing. All signs of shock. Many people think a falling blood pressure is a sign of impending shock. A falling blood pressure is a sign of someone already in shock. If you wait until the blood pressure begins to drop to treat someone for shock you are behind the curve.

At about 15 minutes from the hospital the patient's blood pressure finally starts to fall and he has become difficult to arouse. I have known from the start this patient is hurt very badly. I had hoped to get him to a hospital quick enough to get his internal bleeding stopped. I now realize he may not be alive much longer. I have done everything I can for him. I am trying to keep his blood pressure up with IV fluids but, as I have said, that only buys the patient a few extra minutes. I am giving him high flow oxygen and be ready to intubate if he stops breathing.

I stick my head through the walkway and tell Karen something I very rarely said, "Get us there yesterday!"

Upon arrival at the hospital the patient is still alive but totally unconscious. His abdomen is distended and hard, late evidence of internal bleeding. Breathing is shallow and labored. He died in surgery an hour later.

To see a patient deteriorate before your eyes is upsetting especially when you have done everything you can for them and know it isn't going to help. To see someone go downhill so quickly and die is always hard to take.

Playing Chicken

Team work is an important part of getting the patients of an accident safely out of a vehicle or situation they are in and transported to the hospital in a timely manner. The following couple of stories show this team work in action.

It's about 10:00 P.M. on a cool winter night. A middle aged woman is driving her Cadillac North bound in the South bound lane of a major freeway. Just as she crosses the bridge that separates two neighboring counties she comes head to head with an 18 wheel tanker full of anti-freeze. The driver of the truck would later tell us she made no effort to avoid him in spite of his efforts to get her attention. Being in the middle of the bridge the 18 wheeler had nowhere to go and hit her head on.

The impact ruptures the fuel tanks on the 18 wheeler and within a few moments the diesel fuel catches fire. The fire department is dispatched at the same time we are.

The dispatcher tells us it's a head on collision with vehicles on fire but fails to mention it's an 18 wheeler. The fire department arrives on the scene shortly before we do and reports an 18 wheeler fully involved, fire department slang for "it's really burning." As the scene comes into view David and I see that it's a tanker truck. The fire department's already putting water on it.

"I am going to park down here on the frontage road just in case it blows up," David tells me.

"What difference does it make? If it blows up while we're near it we're dead anyway," I reply fatalistically.

"At least the ambulance will be OK and they'll have something to haul our fat butts to the hospital."

"Makes sense to me," I couldn't argue with that kind of logic.

As we make our way up the small hill towards the wreck we can see the front of the Cadillac wedged under front of the 18 wheeler. A couple of firefighters are getting the "Jaws of Life" ready to pop the doors while others are trying to keep the flames away from the car.

"What's in the tank?" I ask the fire chief.

"Well we don't know actually. Can't find the truck driver or if he's here he hasn't admitted to it," Chief Williams answers anticipating my next question.

Even though the firefighters are making some head way with the fire, smoke is still a problem. The trick for the firefighters is to keep the flames away from the car and the tank at the same time. Not knowing what's in the tank, they don't want to push the flames into it.

A fire fighter pulls on the starter rope several times. The single cylinder motor that turns the hydraulic pump to power the jaws coughs and sputters to life then settles down to a fast idle.

The tips of the Jaws are jammed into the space between the front and back door. The operator pushes the switch to make them open. The "Jaws of Life" is a hydraulic tool that looks somewhat like a giant pair of pliers. The titanium tips can spread open to about 36 inches using tons of hydraulic pressure to force jammed doors open. They are also used to lift and pull other parts of the car apart so rescuers can get to the patients.

David and I wait nearby choking on smoke until the door is forced open. Finally after several cycles of the jaws to get a better bite on the door frame it pops open. Flash lights are shined in and I can see a body wedged under the dash board on the drivers' side. David quickly looks into the rest of the car but can't see any other patients.

She's still breathing but not very well. I feel for and find a weak carotid pulse. The patient is collapsed like an accordion under the dash making any other assessment impossible. I can only assume her legs are broken because they are folded up under her. Just implement of injury leads me to believe she probably has internal injures not to mention spine and neck fractures. She wasn't wearing a seat belt. At the time of this accident there wasn't a law making you wear one. I was actually surprised that she was still alive.

Rapid extrication which is basically grabbing the patient and pulling them out of the situation as quickly as possible is used as a last resort. Paramedics do it when we either have a patient that is in eminent danger of dying from their wounds or in a situation like this where there is a chance of the patient burning up. It doesn't take a rocket scientist to determine that she meets both of these criteria.

"Let's get her out of here," I tell David and Ricky the assistant fire chief.

David grabs under her left arm pit while Ricky gets a hold under her right one. I stabilize her head and count, "One, two, three," we all pull but nothing happens.

We try again with the same results. She's wedged too tightly between the seat and the floorboard.

I turn to the man with the jaws, "Bill, we need to get her out now. Use the jaws to push the seat back."

Bill did as ask and placed the tips between the door frame and the seat and hit the switch. The seat moves a little but then the door frame begins to bend. Bill takes another try with the same results.

During this time David, seeing what is happening notices the button on the side of the car seat that moves it back and forth. On a hunch that saved us a lot of time he reaches down and pushes the button. We are all surprised but happy when the motor kicks in and moves the seat back five or six inches.

"Ok guys let's try this again," I say.

David, Ricky, and I assume our former positions. I nod my head and we try again. The few inches are just enough to get her free. We lay her on a backboard and carry her to the ambulance.

It's about this time that the truck driver decides to make his presence known and inform the chief that the tanker contains anti-freeze. The firefighters have been fighting the fire as if the tanker contained gasoline or some other flammable substance. The driver had been standing at a safe distance with the crowd and didn't volunteer any information until the fire was almost out. I never found out why he did this but the word coward comes to mind. While anti-freeze is not flammable it still could have been dangerous if the tank had ruptured spilling 6,000 gallons on everything.

The patient ended up with a broken femur on one leg and the lower leg broken on the other. The only internal injury she had was a ruptured spleen. All serious injuries but ones she survived. She even started to regain consciousness just before we arrived at the hospital. The fact that she was driving one of the old heavy Cadillac's is probably what saved her.

We never did find out if she did it on purpose or not. Since she didn't smell like she had been drinking I and several others on the scene thought she was more than likely trying to kill herself.

Everyone involved in the call that night except for the deputies were volunteers. Everyone assumed the tanker had a flammable substance in it. No one ran, no one panicked, even though they knew there was a possibility of the tank exploding and killing us all. We had a patient to take care of and we did it. Afterwards we even joked about how David protected the ambulance. Like I said, paramedics need a sense of humor.

Mud Pies

It is early spring in Southeast Texas. It's had been raining all day but quit about the time it became dark.

A young man, just 18 years old, and his 16 year old girl friend are on the phone planning to run away together. She has just had a fight with her parents concerning him and she wanted to leave. At about 11:00 P.M. he pulls up in front of her home. She's waiting by her bedroom window and makes a run for the car as soon as it stops. Her parent's hear the car pull up. They look out the living room window just in time to see her get in and speed away.

Her dad immediately calls the sheriff's department and tells them what happened. The sheriff's dispatcher broadcast a description of the car to the deputies in the field. A deputy patrolling near the parent's home spots the speeding car and attempts to stop it. The car doesn't stop and in fact speeds up. The deputy radios he is in pursuit of the vehicle along with his location and direction of travel. The roads are still wet and slick from the rain earlier that day causing both cars to slip and slide during the chase. As they approach an intersection made muddy by nearby construction the young man loses control and runs off the road into a telephone pole. The impact knocks the girl out but doesn't injure the boy. The deputy pulls up just as the boy runs around the car picks her up and starts running towards the woods he knows are nearby. Unseen by the young man and the deputy is a 25 foot hole in the ground directly in his path.

Workers at that intersection were building a storm sewer system for the new homes to be built in the woods the young man was running towards. Most of the 5 foot diameter pipe had been covered up except for one large hole about 30 foot square and 25 feet deep. The intersection was unlit and since the hole was several yards off the road it was not marked.

As the young man runs with his girlfriend in his arms, the deputy gets out of his patrol car and runs through the mud after them. He is shining his flash light on them when they disappear. He slips and slides to the edge of the hole in time to see the young man scramble into a man hole opening in the pipe. Lying next to the man hole in the mud is the girl, still unconscious. The deputy thinks she's dead and immediately calls for ambulance and rescue.

By the time Theresa and I arrive on the scene, the fire department has already set up flood lights. First responders had arrived quickly and slid down into the hole to find the girl was still unconscious but alive. Someone had already climbed into the manhole and found the young man passed out about 50 yards from the opening.

I look into the abyss and see people attending to the girl. Since she had been unconscious for at least 5 minutes I start to become concerned that she may have a closed head injury.

Three sides of the hole are straight up and down. The fourth one is angled at about 45 degrees. At least we will not have to lift them straight out. I decide to go down to the girl to assess how badly hurt she might be. I stay on my feet for about 5 seconds before falling on my butt and sliding the rest of the way.

While we were responding to the scene the fire department had told us what had happened. I knew she had been in an auto accident and was not wearing a seat belt. I knew she was more than likely unconscious when her boyfriend picked her up and ran. The fall of 25 feet could only make matters worse. I check her out and I am surprised to find no obvious fractures but I am still concerned about possible internal bleeding and head injuries.

While I assessed her, several first responders went into the manhole to extricate the young man. Scott, one of the first responders sticks his head out of the manhole to give me a report.

"Patrick, he's conscious but kinda confused. I can't find anything broken but he's complaining of general pain. Can't imagine why," Scott says sarcastically. He goes on to tell me he needs a c-collar and a stokes basket.

In anticipation of needing them, two stokes baskets had already been lowered into the hole one for my patient and one the young man in the storm sewer. A stokes basket is made out of aluminum tubing and heavy duty wire best described as looking like chicken wire. It is about 6 feet long and is several inches deep. It's narrow at the head and feet and wide in the middle. Roughly shaped like the outline of a person. It is intended to cradle or hold the patient like a basket. The patient is then tied into it. With the patient secured in such a manner you can lift or lower them and they won't fall out. You can even lift them with the basket turned vertically if needed. In the case of the young man in the storm sewer, it was the only way to get him out.

The first responders had not moved the girl. She is still laying on her right side in a fetal position when I examined her.

"Get me two c-collars," I yell up to Theresa.

I had left Theresa up on top for two reasons. One so she someone familiar with our ambulance could get equipment we needed. The other reason is that since I had plenty of help down in the hole one of us needed to stay clean if possible. Moments later she throws them down. I toss one to Scott and he disappears into the manhole.

"Ok guy's let's get her packaged and out of this mud hole," I tell the people around me.

As we apply the c-collar and lift her into the stokes basket, we discuss what will be the best way to lift her out.

260

"Well guys, are we going to try to walk her up the sloped side or are we going to rig ropes to life her out?" I ask.

"If we want to lift her out, it will take time to rig all the stuff to do it with. I think we can get her up the slop if we all try," one of the responders, tells me.

"Ok, let's try to get up the slope. Heck, we're all filthy anyway so what if we do slip and slide a little."

I look around. There are six of us. "Ok, 3 on that side and 3 over her." We lift the stokes basket and start up the slope of mud. In seconds we are all too busy trying to stand up much less carry the stokes basket.

"Ok guys stop. This sure as heck isn't working," I say.

We are all on the verge of laughing out loud because we know how stupid we must look.

Jim calls up to the firefighters, "Get a rope and throw down one end. We'll tie it to the stokes basket and y' all can pull us out."

A rope is thrown down and tied off to the basket and several people start to pull. Even though we are still slipping and sliding within a few moments we manage to make it out.

The girl is still unconscious as we place her in the ambulance; muddy stokes basket and all and put her on the bench. "Theresa gets me a set of vitals. Jim, go see how much longer it will be before they get the boy out. I want to roll as soon as I can. If they are going to be awhile, I am going to transport her and call for another ambulance for the other patient." Jim takes off and I grab a towel to try to wipe some of the mud off my hands.

Theresa finishes with the vitals; they are within normal range. I ask Theresa to hang an IV. I hope that by the time I get an IV established the rescuers will have the boy out and up to the ambulance. When I stick her arm with the needle she responds to the pain and withdraws. I now know that her spinal cord in the cervical region is pretty much intact since she felt the pain in her arms.

Jim returns and tells me they are bringing the boy. As they approach the back of the ambulance I can hear him yelling.

"I told you M----- F------to leave me alone. There ain't nothing wrong with me. I didn't do nothing wrong."

"Ok guys put him right here," I say pointing to the stretcher.

The patient is placed on the stretcher, stokes basket and all. Of course the patient along with the stokes basket is covered in mud. Scott gives me a medical report while the patient continues to maintain his innocence, denying injury, and calling into question everyone's relationship with their mother.

"We found him about 50 feet down the pipe. He was unconscious when I got to him but woke up while we were packaging him and he has been like this ever since. I can't find any obvious injuries. I don't know if his attitude is due to a head injury of if he's just normally an ass," Scott reports.

"Yea, I know what you mean."

Scott is referring to is the fact that head injuries can sometimes alter a patient's behavior and personality. They can become aggressive, irrational, and uncooperative. Determining if it is a head injury or just the patient's normal demeanor is difficult to determine especially if they are drunk. Since patients who are drunk frequently act in the same manner, it is difficult to determine what is causing the behavior. A paramedic has to determine, is it the alcohol or the head injury or is it a combination of both. You always assume it's a head injury until proven otherwise. If your patient doesn't appear to have been drinking, as with this young man, you assume it is a head injury. Since he hit a tree at 40 to 50 mph and then fell 25 feet, I can make the assumption that he has a head injury. It is what paramedics call "implement of injury" which means we expect certain types of injuries from certain types of accidents.

Because they both were in a car wreck and then fell, I expect them to possibly have head, neck, back and internal injuries. I quickly get an IV on the boy and we head for the hospital. Since I have two patients, I commandeer Scott to give me a hand.

I am worried more about the girl since she is still unconscious. I check her pupils again and see they are still equal. In closed head injuries as the brain swells you sometimes see the pupils become uneven but not always. Her vitals remain stable throughout the transport. She finally starts to moan and groan a little just before arrival at the hospital.

As for the young man he continues to cuss and scream the entire trip. Scott and I finally conclude that his behavior is more than likely due to him being a jerk than a head injury. Later we find out we are right. He ends up not having any significant injuries. His girlfriend on the other hand is not as lucky, she ended up with a fractured skull. The good news is she eventually recovered.

I had radioed the hospital we were coming but I did not tell them about the mud. I could see their mouths drop as Theresa, Scott, and I rolled the patients into the ER. There was mud on everything and everyone. The nurse wanted to know why we hadn't cleaned them up. The fact we didn't have access to water didn't seem to matter to her. It was almost like they thought we enjoyed messing up their ER. Truth be known since we were already dirty it was kind of fun to see the nurses get all upset.

Team work made the difference on this call, about twenty people including firefighters and first responders were there. We had the patients out of the hole and ready to transport in less than 20 minutes. Everyone jumped right in without regard to the mess they were getting into.

Know your Territory

It's a cool night in late fall and a sheriff's deputy is attempting to stop a motorcycle for speeding. Instead of pulling over the motorcycle driver decides to make a run for it. For reasons known only to the motorcycle driver he decides to turn off the main road he's on and into a subdivision he isn't familiar with in an attempt to shake the deputy. Unknown to the young man on the motorcycle he turns onto a narrow black top road that dead ends into a small pond. He hits the water at about 60 miles per hour. The motorcycle stops almost immediately but he keeps on going and lands about 30 feet further on in about six inches of cold water.

Sharla and I are watching TV at the station when the pager goes off. The call is located at the edge of our territory so it takes us about 15 minutes to get there. It's in an area that doesn't have first responders so no one is there to provide care prior to our arrival. All we are told is that it's a motorcycle accident with no other vehicles involved.

I pull up to the location and see four patrol cars. We get out of the unit and find the officers standing on the edge of the black top road talking to each other. Being unfamiliar with the area myself I didn't know there was a pond. I am surprised to see water just beyond the end of the road.

"Where's the patient?" I ask since none of the officers seems to be forthcoming with any information.

"He's out there," I am told by one of the officers as he points toward the pond with his flashlight.

"Is he alive?" I ask.

The deputies seem to be so unconcerned I figure the patient is either dead or only sustained minor injuries. I was wrong on both counts.

"He was the last time we hollered at him," replies the deputy in an attempt to be funny.

I shine my flashlight out on to the water and finally see the patient, he roughly 40 feet away laying on his right side in about 6 inches of water. I see the motorcycle, which is also laying the water; it's only 10 feet away.

"Did any of you gentlemen bother to go out and check on him?" I ask being as sarcastic as I can.

"Nope, not my job," one of them shoots back.

Sharla and I exchange annoyed glances as we wade into the pond.

As we wade out to the patient, I call to him and he answers. At least the deputies are right about one thing, he is still alive. I kneel by the patient to examine him while Sharla holds the flashlight.

"What happened?" I ask him.

You can tell a lot by the way a patient answers this question. I, of course, want to know what happened but you can sometimes tell other things about the patient's condition by the way they answer. Obviously you can tell if they are conscious or not. You can see how quickly they respond. If they are slow to answer they might have been knocked out for a period on time. If the patient repeats things you might suspect a concussion or head injury. You can tell by the tone if they appear to be in pain.

"Well I was runnin' from the cops and didn't know this damn lake was here and ran off into it," he answers.

"Do you hurt anywhere?"

"Not really, just my back," then almost like an afterthought he says, "I can't move my legs."

I do a quick head to toe exam and don't see any obvious limb fractures. In a lot of motorcycle accidents you see leg and arm fractures due to the patient rolling and tumbling after they fall off the bike. Of course you always suspect spinal injuries.

When a patient tells you they can't move their legs you immediately go on high alert. I have also learned from experience you clarify their answer by asking a few more questions.

"Can you really not move your leg or does it hurt too badly for you to move them?"

Most of the time you are told that it hurts to move them. In the case of this young man, unfortunately, he tells me he can't move them.

Sharla hears his answer and heads for the ambulance to get the backboard, c-collars, and webbing to secure him. I notice he is starting to shake and shiver from lying in the cold water for over 20 minutes.

You get to know a lot of the officers within your territory you also get to know which ones will help you with a patient and which ones won't. I only knew one of the deputies on the scene and he never attempted to help.

,When Sharla returns with the equipment I call up to the street and ask for help. "Hey, this guy might have a bad back injury. Could we get a couple of you down here to give us a hand?"

I will normally ask a bystander to help with a patient before I will an officer. Since there was no one else on the scene, I had no choice. When the sergeant sees I am serious he orders the rookie to help.

It's funny watching him tip toe out into the pond in an attempt to keep from getting his shinny boots and pants wet. A cuss word accompanies each step. His buddies, still high and dry, are laughing at him as he slowly makes his way toward us.

Sharla, not as good as me at keeping her mouth shut, hollers at the officer, "You're already wet get your ass down here."

Since Sharla was young and cute she could get away with talking to him like that.

I explain to the patient what we are going to do, "I am going to hold your head while Sharla places this brace around your neck to hold it still. Then we are going to roll you carefully onto this board. If you understand say yes. Don't shake your head."

"Yes," he replies.

Even though I had been holding his head and neck still since we got to him I didn't want him to move any more than necessary. Sharla places the c-collar around his neck. I have the deputy hold the board against his back. I hold his head and neck while Sharla rolls him onto the board. The idea is to keep movement of the patients' spine to a minimum. Normally you want at least three people moving the patient and one or two holding the board. In this case we were lucky to have the one extra person so we make do with what we have.

Sharla and I secured him to the board using one inch wide nylon webbing. It's done in a crisscross pattern over the patient with most crews having their own particular way of doing it. If done right, it's a quick and effective way to immobilize and secure a patient to the backboard.

The next big obstacle is to get the patient up and out of the water and into the ambulance. Having found the pond bottom fairly solid I have a brainstorm. Instead of attempting with only three people to carry him out, I have Sharla go get the stretcher and bring it to us in the water. We lift him up and place him on the stretcher and then drag it up to the street as the other officer's watch.

After getting him loaded, I am able to do a better assessment. I do a neurological check to see if he has any sensation in his legs. One test is to run the tip of your scissors up the soles of their feet starting at the heel. A normal reaction is for the patient's toes to curl up. In his case there is no reaction. I quickly assume the patient has some sort of spinal cord or nerve damage. Then I start up the patient's legs pinching them every few inches to check for sensation. He finally says he can feel me touching him just below his waist. In some cases the patient's loss of sensation and movement are temporary due to the spinal cord swelling. I hope this is the case with this patient.

Since he was thrown as far as he was it's a possibility he sustained internal organ injuries as well. With this in mind I check his abdomen for swelling and tenderness which can be signs of internal injury and bleeding. I don't find any other obvious injuries. This is probably due to having landed in the pond.

Now that we are away from the deputies, I am curious to hear the patient's side of the story. As Sharla takes vitals, I start to question him. I already know his name, age, and drug allergies. Asking about allergies is one of the first things a good paramedic should ask a patient upon making contact, followed by name and age. This serves two purposes. Is the patient conscious and alert? If he or she is able to answer at least some of these questions you have established a level of consciousness. The second reason you ask these particular questions is because if patient later becomes unconscious you at least have some basic information about them. Drug allergies are important to know. For instance, if a patient has a seizure the usual drug of choice to give them would be Valium. If you are aware of a patient's allergy to Valium before the seizure it could save their life.

"Well now, tell me how you happened to run off into a lake?" I ask.

The patient had been pretty calm up to this point but becomes somewhat upset at the question.

"If they had just left me alone this wouldn't have happened," he says starting to shout.

"They? Who are they?" I ask.

I assumed he meant the deputies, but I wanted to make sure.

"The damn cops, who else to you think?" he shouts back.

"Did you run from them like they said?"

"You damn right I did."

I was getting curious now.

"Why didn't you just stop and take the ticket?"

"When you've been in as much trouble with the law as I have, you don't want no part of them."

"Did you really think you could get away? And why did you turn down a road that dead ended into a lake?" I figured that while he was confessing all, I would ask.

I had assumed he knew the subdivision he turned into or perhaps lived there and thought he could lose them on the back streets.

"I didn't know there was lake there. I was just running and hoping to get away."

Nothing like a well thought out plan, I think. It was becoming evident that this young man was a couple of bricks shy when it came to smarts.

Just as we are getting ready to head to the hospital one of the deputies opens the back door and asks to talk with the patient.

"He'd been lying out in the lake for 20 minutes before we got here. Why didn't you talk with him then? I ask.

The deputy stares at me blankly. My question has caught him off guard. Before he has a chance to answer I tell him, "Sorry, he needs to get to the hospital now; we were just getting ready to go. If you need to talk to him you can do it at the emergency room." The deputy slams the door. It was great to get the last word.

Quite often when someone has been severely injured it takes a while for them to realize the extent of their injuries. We are about half way to the hospital before the patient begins to realize the lack of movement in his legs might mean he is paralyzed. "Does this mean I'll never walk again?" he asks me.

Since I have no idea how badly his spine might or might not be injured I try to assure him that until further test are done there is no reason to jump to conclusions.

"If I'm crippled I'm gonna sue those bastards for everything they got," the patient shouts at no one in particular.

The fact that it was his decision to run seemed to escape his logic.

Unfortunately this young man was permanently injured and paralyzed as a result of this accident. I wonder if he ever realized that being hasseled by the cops would have been much less trouble than spending the rest of his life in a wheelchair.

Quick Decision

The first responders have already told us we have three critical patients. I radio dispatch and tell them to roll a second unit and put life flight on standby. Dispatch calls back a few moments later and informs me Lifeflight is on standby but only one chopper is available.

We approach dead man's curve. I would venture to guess almost every rural county has one, so named because of it being a blind or sharp curve and causing an unusually high number of bad accidents. This curve was no different.

Jason weaves around the fire trucks and patrol cars and comes to a stop along-side an upside down red Jeep Cherokee. The car is sideways across the ditch. Illuminated by flood lights, I see several first responders crawling in and out of the jeep with equipment. As another is tending to a woman lying beside the Jeep.

I step out of the ambulance and hear several people calling my name. Kathy who is tending to the woman motions for me to come over to her. John is inside the jeep and is yelling for me to come help him.

"Jason go check out Kathy's patient. I'm going over here," I say pointing to the jeep.

The Jeep looks as if it has rolled several times. The driver's side "A" post is bent and the roof is collapsed all along where the front windshield should have been. The tailgate is open and I can see several people inside. John, the first responder, is tending to a middle aged man lying on the ceiling in the back of the upside down Jeep. I kneel down by the opening to get a better look. The man is conscious and lying on his right side.

"What have you got?" I ask John as I do my usual head to toe once over.

"I don't think anything's broken, he seems to be breathing ok," John answers hesitantly.

The first thing I notice are his legs, they don't appear to be broken but they are intertwined at an odd angle. I am extremely curious as to why someone would leave their legs in this position if they didn't need to. There are only two reasons I can think of. One is they are so badly broken he can't or fears moving them. Or he has a spinal injury preventing movement. I choose to immediately check for factures. I run my hands over them and find, just as John said, no evidence of them being broken. I now suspect he may have a spinal cord injury. I grab his left thigh and squeeze as hard as I can.

"Sir, move your foot on the leg I'm touching."

"Which foot do you want me to move?" he asks.

"The left one," I tell him still squeezing.

I don't see any movement at all.

"Is it moving?"

"Do you hurt anywhere?" I ask quickly, avoiding his question.

"No not really. Can I get up now?"

At this moment John and I realize, that the patient probably has spinal cord injuries.

"No, you need to stay here for a little while. We'll get you out in a few minutes."

I grab his hands and tell him to squeeze. His right hand moves a little, the left one doesn't move at all. This tells me his spinal injury is either in the lower cervical or high thoracic region of his spine.

"Were you wearing your seat belt?" I know the answer to this question before he even tells me.

"No."

"How did you end up in the back of the car?" I wanted to know if he was thrown there or had crawled there before he became paralyzed.

"I ended up here, I guess."

"John, go get the KED. I'll be back."

As I finish checking the paralyzed patient, Carl another first responder motions for me to come to the front of the Jeep. Laying under the hood but not trapped by it was another middle aged man. I could only assume he had been thrown out through the missing windshield.

"What have you got?"

I can see this patient moving his arms and the one leg that wasn't broken. He is conscious but the smell of whiskey on his breath was all too obvious.

"The only thing I can find is a broken femur," replies Carl.

After doing a quick check, I come to the same conclusion.

"Get someone to help you get a traction splint on him."

I get up and head over to Jason to get a report on the woman. I have already decided I need another ambulance and that I am going to use Lifeflight for the paralyzed man.

"What have you got?" I ask Jason.

Just like the other two patients I can smell whiskey on her breath. Unlike the others she is yelling.

"Get you f---ing hands off me and let me up," she shouts.

"Do you recognize who this is?" Jason asks me over her shouts.

I take my first real look at her face and realize she is one of the owners of a convenience store Jason and I sometimes stop at to refuel the ambulance and buy soft drinks and snacks. Jason, who has grown up in the area, has known her since he was a small child. I only know her from the small talk we engage in when I go into her store. She has always been, at least in my opinion, an obnoxious, disagreeable, and argumentative person.

"Yea, I know who she is."

"I think she may have a head injury by the way she is acting."

Jason is right, head injuries often make people act aggressively and uncooperatively. The problem is, so does alcohol. When someone has been in an accident especially one where there is a possibility of head injuries and they have been drinking it becomes extremely difficult to determine if there actions are due to injury or drinking or a combination of both.

"Kathy, how was she when you got here?"

Kathy, who also knows her personally, answers, "She was up walking around. She even recognized me. She said she was driving the Jeep and swerved to avoid a cow when the wreck happened. She told me she crawled out of the car after they wrecked. I don't think she was wearing a seatbelt, probably hung on to the wheel."

"Was she acting like this?"

"Yea, pretty much," is Kathy's reply.

"Jamie, it's me Patrick. Can you tell me if you are hurting anywhere?" I have to ask her twice to get her attention before she answers me.

"I keep telling you mother f------- I'm ok."

"How much have you had to drink?"

"I ain't had a damn thing to drink."

Before checking Jamie, I had decided to fly the man that was more than likely paralyzed. Now that I suspect a possible closed head injury I consider flying her instead. Having only one air ambulance available I have to make the difficult decision as to which one to fly.

Although Jamie has the classic signs of a head injury I am nagged by the thought that except for being drunk she is pretty much the same rude disagreeable person I know from the store.

Since I am the medical person in charge, I have to make the decision based on what I can see, information collected from the other medical people on the scene, and my experience. Based on all this I rate the patients in order of the severity of their injuries. As it stands now, the paralyzed man is the most critical, he will go by Lifeflight. The man with the broken femur is the second most injured, he will go by the first ambulance to get to the scene. And finally the woman, who at this time I considered to be the least injured, she can go with the second ambulance to get to us.

When you triage a scene with multiple patients you constantly reassess their condition. You modify your plan if their status changes. My plan is to reassess all the patients when the first ambulance arrives. If her condition changes for the worse I will fly her and send the paralyzed man in the first available ambulance.

"Jason, let's get another unit out here and launch the bird."

"Are we going to fly her?" ask Jason.

"No, there's a guy in the Jeep that's paralyzed. I want to fly him. The other one has a femur fracture he can go by Medic 6. I sense Jason disagrees with me but doesn't say anything. He goes to the radio and tells dispatch what we need.

I tell Kathy to let me know if Jamie takes a turn for the worse and to start getting her immobilized. I go back to reassess the others. John has gotten the KED and is attempting to put it on the paralyzed man. KED stands for Kendrick Extrication Device. It is made of vinyl with vertical ribs for support with straps to assist in moving a patient with a back injury. It wraps around the patient from just below their waist past their head. You secure it using several buckles and straps that go around the patient's thighs to prevent them from slipping when they are lifted. It more or less cocoons them, hopefully preventing further injury to their spine.

Medic 6 arrives on the scene. Jim, one of our newer paramedics, quickly finds me and asks what I want him to do.

"That guy over there has a broken femur," I say pointing to the front of the jeep, "He's yours."

I know Jim will be able to handle him and I won't have to worry about that patient.

Jason gets out of the unit and lets me know Lifeflight and a third ambulance is on the way. He stops to tell Carlos, the DPS officer, that Lifeflight is coming before heading over to help Kathy. I can still hear Jamie telling her to leave her alone.

I turn my attention back to the paralyzed patient.

"Dan we're going put this behind you. It will help us get you out of here, OK," I show him the KED as I explain.

But why can't I just get up?" he asks, still appearing to be unaware of his paralysis.

"Well, this is just in case something is hurt or broken that we aren't aware of. It keeps us from making the injury worse," I explain.

I have only treated a few patients who were already paralyzed when I arrived on the scene. The common thing for all of them, at least for a while, is they didn't seem to be aware of their paralysis. When they do finally realize it, varying degrees of panic set in. I keep expecting Dan to suddenly realize the extent of his injuries, but as of yet he has not. I feel it is probably due to his consumption of Jack Daniels earlier.

John and I carefully slide the KED under Dan and secure him to it. It takes several minutes but we are finally ready to have others help us get him out of the jeep and into my ambulance. Meanwhile Jason and Kathy along with the assistance of several firefighters have finally wrestled Jamie onto a backboard.

I yell at the firefighters, "When you guys finish your wrestling match would you come over here and give us a hand?"

John and I slowly slide and wiggle Dan so his head is pointing out the back of the Jeep. We then maneuver the backboard as close as we can and start to slide him on to it. The firefighters are securing the back board and, as Dan gets within their reach, they start to carefully pull him onto it. Kind of like a bucket brigade. Once on the board, we secure Dan to it and place him on the stretcher. I ask John and the others to take him to my ambulance. I want to check make a quick check on Jamie.

"Any changes?" I ask Jason and Kathy.

"No not really," Jason tells me, "I guess you heard the fight to get her immobilized?"

"Yea, I did," I answer.

Jason continues, "She still seems to pretty much know who we are and what's going on. Her pupils are equal and reactive and she denies she was knocked out. It's just that she's so hard to control. I still think she might have a closed head injury."

"I agree," states Kathy, "she just isn't acting right."

I hear the third ambulance's siren in the distance and know I need to make a final decision as to who gets to fly and who doesn't. I kneel down and attempt to talk with Jamie one more time. After getting cussed at instead of answers, I make a final decision that she is not really injured that badly. I decide she is just a mean drunk and will go by ground.

On the other hand I know Dan has a definite spine injury. If he has any hope at all of walking again going by helicopter to a level 1 trauma center instead of a bouncy ambulance might be his only chance.

"When Medic 5 gets here let them have Jamie. I'm going to get the other one ready for Lifeflight."

I head for my ambulance but am stopped by the fire chief. He informs me the fire department is setting up a landing zone in a cow pasture next to the cemetery across the street. I always thought it was ironic that dead man's curve was in front of a church and cemetery. He also tells me Lifeflight is 10 minutes away. I thank him as I get in the back on my unit.

"How you doing Dan? We're going to send you to the hospital in the helicopter ambulance. First we have to start an IV."

"Why can't I just go home? I feel ok."

Dan is still unaware of the fact he can't move. I feel I need to at least, to some degree, inform him of the seriousness of his injuries. Before I do and while John is hanging the IV, I do another neurological exam. The results are the same as before.

"Dan, listen to me. I think you may be hurt pretty bad. That's why you are going in the helicopter. You need to go to

Herman hospital in Houston. They specialize in treating people with your type of injury."

I was trying to let him know he was hurt without telling him everything.

"But I don't feel hurt, I don't feel anything," The last word trailed off as Dan finally starts to realize why he didn't feel anything.

Then he asks, "Why don't I feel anything? Is something broken? Is it my back?"

I interrupt him, "Listen Dan you probably injured your back when the Jeep rolled over. I have no way of knowing how bad it is. The hospital will have to take x-rays to find out."

Probably because he is still drunk Dan seems to take the news fairly well. I start an IV, meanwhile John has already put him on oxygen.

I can hear Lifeflight landing as Roy, the paramedic on medic 5, appears at the back door of my ambulance.

"Are you sure you want me to take her to the hospital by ground? I think she has a bad head injury and needs to go by Lifeflight."

Roy and I have never gotten along. He is always argumentative and one of those paramedics who just gets by. If he can get out of a call he will do it. If he can just sit and watch a patient instead of doing real care he will do it. I know the only way to get through to him is by being blunt.

"Listen Roy, I've made my decision. There is only one bird available and he is going on it. She's a loud mouth drunk that you should be able to handle. Now get going."

"You're screwing up man," with that said Roy turns around and leaves.

The nurse from Lifeflight comes to the back door few moments later. I give her a rundown of Dan's condition and after she does her own neuro exam comes to the same conclusion I have.

"Well let's get him loaded, there's nothing else we can do here," says Tracey. She has been a flight nurse for many years and we have made many calls together.

Within ten minutes of landing Lifeflight has lifted off and is on its way to Herman hospital with Dan. All that is left is to do is a quick clean up and get back in service.

Jason and Kathy express to me that they hope Jamie is really just drunk.

"Listen y' all, I understand your concern but I had to make a decision and I made it."

Hearing both of them second guess me along with Roy is starting to make me wonder if I had in fact screwed up.

Jason speaks up when he realizes I am upset at everyone criticizing my decision.

"Well Pat, I've never seen you mess up yet on triage. I don't know why I'm second guessing you now."

"Thanks. Well let's get back in service we're the only unit in the county now."

While driving back to the station I hear Medic 5 radio they have arrived at the hospital. We have only been back at the station a few minutes when the phone rings. It's Roy.

"Man you royally screwed up. It was all I could do to keep her awake by the time we got to the hospital. I wouldn't be surprised if she dies. She was barely hanging on when we left."

"You can't be serious. What do you mean she was barely hanging on?" I know Roy exaggerates so I wanted him to give me specifics as to what had happened.

"They were getting ready to intubate her man. I telling you, you should have flown her. I'm thinking about calling Medical Control and tell them what you did."

I know Roy has to be exaggerating but what really makes me upset is the threat to turn me in to Medical Control. Even though I can justify my actions the fact that a mediocre paramedic has the gall to act like he has never screwed up makes my blood boil. I slam the phone down rather that to argue with an idiot.

"Who was that?" asks Jason, "Don't tell me, let me guess Roy."

"Yes, damn 90 day wonders, think they know it all," I yell at no one in particular.

"Why don't you call the hospital and check on her, they're bound to know something by now," suggests Jason.

I pick up the phone and dial the emergency room. Debbie, a nurse I know, answers the phone.

"Debbie, this is Patrick I just wanted to check on the status of the female patient Medic 5 brought you a while ago."

"Are you talking about that obnoxious foul mouthed drunk? If you are she's getting ready to leave AMA and not a moment too soon."

AMA means against medical advice.

Relived she was nowhere near "death" as Roy had described I ask Debbie what injuries they had found.

"Other than being one of the most disagreeable patients I have seen in a while and being shit faced drunk, none. Doctor Gant is writing the discharge now. He's also tired of her foul mouth."

I thank her for the information and immediately dial Medic 5's cell phone. I can't wait to tell Roy the good news.

"Hey Roy, I just called the hospital to check up on Jamie and guess what?" I continue before he has a chance to answer. "She being discharged as we speak. The only thing wrong with her is a crappy personality and too much to drink." I pause to let Roy's dim wit brain soak in what I said.

Roy stammers a moment and says meekly, "Well that's good to hear."

"What do you mean that's good to hear? Just a little while ago you called to tell me how much I screwed up and that she was near death. Doesn't it bother you that you are so incompetent that you thought she was near death when in fact she was only drunk just like I told you? To put it into words you can understand. I was right, you were wrong." I then hung up the phone. I had made my point.

Within a week Jamie was back working at the store, just as mean and disagreeable as ever. Dan died about a month after the accident. People close to him said he just gave up after coming to the realization he was a quadriplegic. The other patient recovered. Roy avoided me after that but his career ended a few months later when he was accused of sexually assaulting a fellow female employee.

Chapter 10....Man Down

A "man down" call can be anything and of course it includes "women down." Most of the time there is not much to it, a drunk in the ditch or a homeless person just trying to sleep. Of course it can be someone nearly beat to death or shot. Sometimes it's a medical condition such as a stroke or a diabetic emergency.

Nap Time

Several motorists are standing around a man lying on his back in the grassy median between the freeway and the access road. As we approach I do my usual head to toe survey. No outward signs of injury and he's breathing.

"What happened?" I ask the crowd as I kneel down beside the patient.

"I was driving by and saw him lying here and stopped to see what was wrong. I shook him but he didn't move so I called for the ambulance. I think he was riding that motorcycle up there," an elderly man tells us pointing toward the shoulder of the freeway.

I look up and see an old BSA motorcycle parked on the side of the road. The man is laying about 20 feet from it. Keeping a foot or so distance between me and the patient, you never know when they will come up swinging. I reach over, grab his shoulder and shake it. He doesn't move. I shake a little harder, still nothing. Jerry reaches down and checks for a pulse.

"Strong and regular," he tells me.

"I don't smell booze either," I say as I shake him again, this time causing his whole body to move.

He still doesn't react. I make a fist and rub my knuckles up and down his sternum. This is called painful stimuli. If you don't believe me try in on yourself, it hurts.

I rub several times pushing harder each time. I am just about ready to treat him as an unconscious-unknown when he starts to move. You treat someone as an unconscious unknown when, as in this situation, you can't wake them up and you don't know why. You assume they are either a drug overdose or are having a diabetic emergency such as insulin shock. You can rule out insulin shock by checking their blood sugar with a glucometer.

In him I didn't have to do this. He finally starts blinking and with some effort opens his eyes. He sits up and looks around at everyone standing around him.

"What's going on?" he asks.

"We couldn't wake you up. Everyone thought something was wrong with you. Are you OK?" I ask, even though he appears to be fine.

"Man I don't need any help. I been on the road all day and got sleepy. I pulled over to rest before I had a wreck," he explains.

"You must be real tired; it took me about a minute to wake you up."

"Yea, I'm a pretty sound sleeper. Well I guess I'll be going."

With that said he stands up puts his helmet on gets on his motorcycle and leaves.

Stop and Go

"Man down" at the Stop and Go could be just about anything, a robbery gone bad, a customer slipping on a wet floor, stomach cramps caused by eating a hot dog from the warmer, or a countless number of other things. As usual details are vague.

Theresa pulls into the parking lot. We are glad to see a sheriff's deputy already there just in case it is a robbery. We walk into the convenience store to find about ten people gathered around the checkout stand. Everyone starts talking at once but it's clear our patient is behind the counter.

"It's the clerk," someone says.

"He just passed out," says someone else.

"I think he had a seizure," says yet another person.

"He handed me my change and just hit the floor," says a middle aged man.

The clerk, a young man in his twenties, is lying on the floor. A young woman is kneeling down beside him holding his hand. We see he is breathing but it is somewhat labored. Theresa checks his pulse while I get the blood pressure cuff out of the kit.

"Hey, look," says Theresa holding up the patients arm, "He's wearing a medic alert bracelet, it says he's a diabetic."

"That's a place to start," I tell her.

I do a sternum rub and finally get him to moan just a little bit. Theresa gets the glucometer to see just how low his blood sugar has dropped. He has all the classic signs and symptoms of being in insulin shock. Which are for the most part the same as any other kind of shock, pale cool moist skin, shallow breathing, unresponsive, or at the very least confused.

With diabetics it's a balancing act to keep their blood sugar level at around 100. On people without diabetes your pancreas regulates the amount of insulin in your body according to how much and what kind of food you have just eaten. With an insulin dependent diabetic their pancreas has quit working so they have to take injections of insulin, usually in the morning and evening. After taking the insulin they need to eat certain amounts of certain foods in an attempt to keep their blood sugar at around a 100. The usual scenario with a diabetic emergency is the patient has taken their morning shot of insulin but forgot to eat breakfast or didn't eat enough. The insulin is in their blood stream waiting to process the sugars produced by the food they didn't eat. A couple of hours later, usually around noon or so, the patient's sugar level drops. When it gets to around 50 or so the patient starts to get confused and disoriented. Many times they are accused of being drunk. Depending on the person they will usually pass out when it gets to about 30. This is considered a life threatening emergency because when blood sugar drops to below 10 the patient's heart can stop.

When the opposite happen it's called a diabetic coma. This is a much slower process. The patient either forgets to take their insulin or eats more than they should. Gradually their blood sugar rises. The difference is that the blood sugar level can get to over 300 or so before the patient has any real symptoms it might get to 600 or so before they actually pass out. Most have gone to the doctor before this because they just aren't feeling good.

He doesn't even flinch when I prick his finger to get blood for the glucometer. In less than a minute it gives us a reading of 20. We quickly get to work. While Theresa gets the IV set up I look for a vein. You have to be careful with diabetics sometimes their veins are brittle which makes it difficult to get a good IV established. I find a good vein and quickly get the IV established.

Theresa hands me the D50W, which stands for fifty percent dextrose in water. It's basically syrup in an injectable form. Since his blood sugar level is extremely low we just inject sugar directly into the patient's blood stream. As with just about all insulin shock patients, he is wide awake within a minute. It is an amazing thing to witness no matter how many times I see it.

The assembled audience is duly impressed to see this young man go from pale and unconscious to awake and alert in a few moments.

I look up and see their faces and can't resist saying, "Neat, huh."

"What did you give him?" asks one.

"Just a little sugar," I tell them.

An emergency room doctor I knew always referred to it as, "Laying on the hands," Which is the best description I have ever heard.

It Ain't The Heat It's The Humidity.

A man covered in paint is lying face down in the yard of a middle class home in the suburbs. As I approach him, I see a scaffold on the side of the house. Another man, also covered in paint, is standing beside his fallen partner.

"He fell from there," he says pointing to the scaffold, "I think he broke his arm."

I see the patient's right forearm is angled somewhat and is probably broken. I also notice he is not moving, a bit unusual for someone who only fell eight feet or so. Unless he landed on his neck or head.

"Did he land on his head when he fell?" I ask the other painter as I kneel down to check for a pulse.

"No, he landed on his side."

The first thing I notice when I touch the patient is he is extremely hot. His skin feels like he just came out of an oven. I am starting to get the idea that this man is suffering from heat stroke and that his broken arm is the least of his worries.

"Did he slip and fall or did he pass out before he fell?" I ask the other painter.

He stops and thinks a second, "He kinda just collapsed and rolled off now that you mention it."

This information added to the 98 degree temperature that day and the patient being unconscious with skin so hot you can barely touch it, all points to heat stroke. An extremely serious and life threatening condition where the patient's body has lost its ability the cool itself. It's kind of like when a car's radiator runs out of coolant. The first treatment is to cool the patient down as quickly as possible.

Brenda, my partner that day, has been standing beside me waiting for me to tell her what to do. She was a part timer who had a heart of gold, but never did learn to anticipate what her partner was doing or needed. Rather than make a mistake, she always waited for directions.

"Brenda, turn that hose on and hand it to me," I tell her pointing to the garden hose hanging on the side of the house.

I get a bewildered look, but she goes over get the hose and brings it to me.

"He's got heat stroke. Go get the stretcher and immobilization stuff." I tell her as I start to hose him down.

She now realizes how serious it is and understands what I am doing and takes off to get the equipment I requested.

We quickly immobilize the patient and get him to the somewhat air-conditioned ambulance. In the middle of Summer in southeast Texas it difficult to cool anything completely. Brenda grabs two instant ice packs from the supply cabinet and activates them by hitting the bag of fluid inside and shaking. She places them on the patient's neck over his carotid artery. This is to assist in cooling his blood, which in turn will cool him down.

I take a quick axillary temperature using our cheap digital thermometer. It reads "Hi" which means somewhere over 104 degrees. We head to the hospital and I establish an IV. His condition remains unchanged as we get him into the trauma room.

The first thing the ER staff does is take a rectal temperature with a more reliable thermometer.

"It's 107," says the nurse.

We all know this is bad. Even if he does live he will have brain damage.

Unfortunately this young man lingered for about a week before he died.

Dehydration is more than likely the cause of this man's death. If he had been more aware of how much water is needed to keep someone hydrated in near 100 degree weather he probably would have survived.

Time Flies When You're Having Fun

On this particular day the information we have from dispatch concerning our "woman down" is that the she is elderly and was found lying in her backyard by a family member. We have also been informed she is conscious.

"At least it's not a full arrest," I say to no one in particular, but since Jason is the only other person in the ambulance he nods his head in agreement.

We had already worked a full arrest earlier that day and didn't really want to work another one but in this business you never know what is around the corner.

"Yea, one a day is enough," Jason answers.

"That reminds me of Black Wednesday. We had 10 full arrests in one 24 hour shift. Have I ever told you about that day?" I ask Jason knowing full well I have.

It's one of those stories that I like to embellish. Truth be known, I did work three full arrests on that day. In addition, I had two more patients that had been dead long enough that I didn't work them. It was a long challenging shift.

Jason rolls his eyes, "Not the Black Wednesday story again. The first time I heard it, you had only 3 full arrests in one shift. Now we're up to 10. I suppose you're going to tell me there was 3 feet of snow on the ground and you had to start a bonfire to unthaw your patient."

"Three feet of snow, don't be silly. We're in South East Texas. It was only two feet of snow. Lucky for you, we are almost there or I would bore you with the whole sorted story."

"Right, lucky me."

Jason picks up the microphone and radios dispatch we are on location. He pulls into the driveway where a middle aged man is flagging us down. The house is an old wood frame painted white with black shutters. I pass it several times a week going to and from work and have always admired how well kept it is.

As we get the equipment out the man starts to tell us what happened, "It's my Mother-in-Law. She's in the back yard. My wife hadn't heard from her in a few days. We came over to check on her and found her in the backyard."

I round the corner of the house and see an elderly woman wearing a plain blue cotton dress lying face down in the grass. Her daughter is kneeling next to her holding her hand. As I kneel beside them I see the patient is conscious and talking. I notice she is moving her right arm and leg but also see she is not moving her left arm and leg. I suspect she has had a stroke.

"Well young lady, what in the world happened to you?"

I always address the patient first. It serves two purposes. First it shows respect for the patient. A lot of medical people from nurses, medics, to doctors address the patient's family members first. This is especially true if the patient is older. I guess they assume the patient is not capable of answering. How do you know the patient is not capable of answering if you don't ask them first? This leads me to the other reason for questioning the patient first. You can determine quickly if they are alert or confused. Even if they are confused, they can still provide you with some information regarding their status.

"Well I was going to the garage to get the lawn mower. My leg gave out and I fell. I couldn't get up so I laid here till someone found me."

She looks at her daughter after telling me this. During this time Jason has checked her for obvious fractures and did not find any.

"This is a heck of a place to take a nap. How long have you been laying here?" I ask.

"Oh, dear I've been here for three days now. I just couldn't get up. I've been yelling for help, but no one heard me."

I am shocked to hear her answer and at first don't know if she is confused or not. Her daughter looks at me and shakes her head in disbelief. We both think she is confused as to how long she has been in the back yard.

Like most people that have had a stroke, she seems to not be aware that she cannot move her left arm and leg. She realizes she can't get up but doesn't know why.

"Mam, are you sure you've been here for three days?" I had to ask again just to make sure.

"I've seen the sunrise and fall three times since I fell. I tell you I've been here three days."

"OK, I was just making sure. Jason is going to check your blood pressure and ask some questions. I'll be back in a second."

I stand up and motion the daughter to step away with me. She is even more upset than when we first arrived. I suspect guilt from not checking on her mother sooner. I am right.

"How could I be so stupid? Why didn't I check on her sooner? Is she going to be Ok?" she asks me frantically.

"I think she is going to make it, but I have to ask you something. Has she had a stroke in the past? I don't know if you've noticed or not but she is not moving her left arm or leg."

"No, she's never had a stroke before, I didn't even notice her arm not moving. "

"I think she had a stroke as she was walking across the yard. I also think she has been laying there for almost 4 days," the daughter recoils. I go on to explain, "If she has seen the sun rise and set three times since falling and she fell in the morning that means she has been here for over three days."

"Oh my goodness how could she just lay there for four days. I can't believe I didn't check on her. Do you think she's going to be alright?"

"I am surprised she is doing as well as she is, all things considered, but I do think she's had a stroke. That's serious enough. I really don't know the long term effect of being outside for several days. We'll just have to take her to the hospital and see what happens."

I didn't want to get the daughter's hopes up too much because I really didn't know how she would do in the long term.

Jason is just finishing up with the vitals and I turn my attention back to the patient.

"What did you get?" I ask Jason.

"Well all the vital are pretty good BP is 140 over 90, everything else is normal," he replies. "Do you want to c-collar and backboard her?"

"Yea, go ahead."

As Jason heads to the ambulance to get the immobilization equipment, I kneel back down to talk with the patient.

"Emma, we are going to take you the hospital. Because you fell we're going to have to roll you on to a hard wooden board. Ok?"

"Whatever you say, I ain't going nowhere by myself."

I was glad to hear she still had her sense of humor. Her daughter even laughed a little. While I waited, I leaned over and grabbed her left hand.

"Emma, can you squeeze my hand with your left hand?" I asked her.

"Why sure," she answers.

I wasn't surprised when nothing happened. I just wanted to make sure she couldn't move it. There again she didn't seem to notice it didn't move.

"Emma do you hurt anywhere?"

"No not really."

"Are you cold?"

"No not really."

"When's you birthday?"

"September 23rd."

I am more concerned about her mental status than I want to admit to her daughter. Even though Emma is able to give me the right answers to the typical questions of birthday and name she seemed to be detached from the fact she has been laying in her backyard for several days. I figure that is her way of dealing with the situation.

Jason returns with the immobilization equipment and we quickly prepare to roll Emma onto the backboard. The object when doing this is to keep the patient's spine as straight as possible while several people roll the patient over and on to the backboard. The person holding the patient's head is always the one to call cadence. I am at her head, Jason and the patient's son-in-law are ready to roll her.

"Ok Emma here we go, one, two, three."

I hold her head in line as she is rolled onto her back. Even though she had told me how long she had laid on the ground, I had hoped it really hadn't been that long. I am taken aback to see the grass under her has turned completely yellow. I know immediately she has been there at least two or three days and possibly longer.

Jason and the patient's family also see the color of the grass and are as shocked as I am. The temperature at night had been in the 60's. Considering she had spent two or three nights exposed, I am amazed she is not hypothermic. I am also amazed she is as lucid as she is. I start an IV, knowing she must be dehydrated. During transport I continue to monitor her vitals and mental condition. I am concerned about her long term survival. She is 82 years old and has probably suffered a massive stroke. The fact that she survived up to this point is nothing short of a miracle.

I usually didn't follow up on most patients other than to ask how they did the next time I went to the emergency room. In the case of Emma I did check on her progress several times in the next few weeks. I was happy to find out that not only did she live through her ordeal; she made some progress in regaining some use of her leg and arm.

Chapter 11....Odds and Ends

Boys Will be Boys

"He's in the back seat. Little twerp won't tell us what happened." The deputy tells us pointing to his patrol car. Susan and I walk over and open the door. A young man is sitting there wrapped in a white sheet.

"What happened?" Susan asks.

"I can't tell you," he replies timidly without looking at us.

I see what could be superficial a knife wound on his upper right shoulder. He is a thin older teenager who obviously doesn't want to talk about what happened to him.

Susan tries another tactic. She takes his hand and, in her best motherly voice, tells him.

"I know you're upset. What if we get you into the ambulance and out of this crowd?"

He shakes his head yes but still doesn't make eye contact. I go get the stretcher as the patient with Susan's insistence and assistance gets out of the patrol car and sits on it. As we roll him to the ambulance I can hear a neighbor talking to deputies about what she saw.

"I heard screams and looked out to see him running around in his yard naked screaming for help. I've known him since he was a little kid so I ran over to see what was wrong. All he would say was that someone stabbed him. I tried to get him to come in the house and sit down, but he wouldn't. I came in and called 911."

Susan also hears this and asks the patient if it is true. He barely manages to shake his head yes. He is responding more to a Susan than to me so I let her continue to talk with him after putting him in the ambulance. I sit in the captain's chair while Susan takes vitals and checks for more wounds. The one I spotted originally is very superficial. I'm beginning to think this is more of a feel sorry for me call than anything else.

"I'm afraid to tell the cops what happened. They'll laugh at me," he finally says to Susan.

He seems to have forgotten I am in the ambulance.

"What did happen?" Susan asks in her most compassionate voice.

"Well, my mom and dad are on vacation. I went to Galveston and brought someone home. We were in bed having fun when he started choking me," He pauses and sobs a few times then continues, "I kicked him until he let go. Then he grabbed a piece of wood doweling and started hitting me with it. It broke and he tried to stab me with the broken end. That's how I got the cut. I ran from him. That's when the neighbor saw me."

"What happened to the guy?" asks Susan.

"He chased me outside then ran away," he explains between more sobs.

"What did he look like?" Susan queries him further.

"He's about my age, 18 or so, and has blond hair. I think he was only wearing his underwear."

I have all the information I need and go out the side door to tell the deputies. Just as the patient predicted they all find the story quite amusing. The sergeant radios the dispatcher and gives her a description of the assailant. A few moments later an APB is broadcast to be on the lookout for an older teenager possible only wearing underwear.

I let Susan ride with the patient since she has gained his confidence. About 10 minutes later I hear a deputy radio he is stopping a suspicious person walking down the freeway in his underwear trying to hitchhike.

While the patient in this story wasn't hurt too badly, it could have been a lot worse. Picking up a stranger and bringing him home may have been an adventure for this young man but if he hadn't escaped there is no telling what may have happened.

A lot of young people have been killed after meeting up with strangers. He was lucky.

Bad for Business

Karl's Grocery is a ma and pa gas station, grocery and liquor store located at the cross roads of a major intersection in eastern Grimes county. This is where a lot locals in this very rural area buy the "essentials" of life, beer, cigarettes, and lotto tickets.

A white Chevy extended cab pickup comes to a screeching halt in front of the store. The driver, a young man, and his equally young wife jump out and run into the store yelling for someone to call 911.

Kathy and Jim, both first responders who live in the area, are there within a few minutes. The only information we have from the dispatcher is a "possible heart attack" at the store.

Jason and I arrive about 10 minutes after Kathy and Jim. I notice a small group gathered around a white pickup. As I get out, I can see Kathy leaning into the truck and go over to see what is going on. I get to the door and see Jim in the back seat trying to lift someone. Kathy is doing her best to help him lift the patient and get her out of the back seat of the extended cab truck. Being an older model extended cab it doesn't have separate door for the back. It is like a two door car. You have to pull the front seat forward and climb over.

Jason and I immediately lend a hand, but even with the four of us, it takes a couple of minutes to get the heavy set lifeless woman out of the back of the truck.

"I tried to get someone to help when we first got here," explains Kathy as we struggle to get the woman out of the truck, "No one moved a muscle."

"Is there any family around?" Jason asks.

"Her son and daughter-in-law are in the store."

We are all huffing and puffing by the time we get the patient out and lay her on the side walk in front of the store. I already know she didn't have a pulse when Kathy arrived. Since it was impossible to start CPR until we got her out, she has been in full arrest for at least 10 to 15 minutes, far too long to attempt resuscitation. Jason hooks up the monitor, but we all know she will be straight line.

"Why in the world was she in the back seat?" I ask, but of course no one knows the answer.

"I guess I'll go in and tell the family. Jason, call the dispatcher so we can get the judge out to pronounce her dead."

I go in to the small cafeteria in front of the store were her Son is sitting and inform him his mother is dead. After a few minutes of conversation with him I find out the rest of the story. His mother, who was only 55 years old, was complaining of chest pain at home. Instead of calling for the ambulance they decide to drive her to the hospital. He told me that she had gone unconscious several minutes before they arrived at the store. I wanted to ask him why he thought it was a good idea to make a sick woman climb into the back of a truck but didn't. I conclude that the combined IQ of him and his wife would probably only add up to 60.

I go back outside to wait for law enforcement and the judge to arrive. Kathy has covered the deceased with a sheet but seeing a dead body lying beside the front door of the store draws a bit of attention as customers arrive. To my surprise most customers still go on in.

One man gets out of his truck and doesn't spot the body until he starts to open the store door. He suddenly stops.

"Well I was going to buy a lottery ticket but this store doesn't seem to be having a good day," with that said he get in his truck and drives off.

Fear of Snakes

Its late afternoon, a deputy has requested an ambulance to be dispatched to his location non-emergency.

"This is never good," I tell my inexperienced partner.

"Why's that?" asks Robert.

"It usually means the deputy doesn't know what to do with whoever he's dealing with. Probably gave them the old ultimatum."

"The ultimatum?"

"Yea, cops love to use it when they really don't want to arrest someone. They say, 'You can either go the hospital or you can go to jail.' "Or something along those lines."

It's dusk by the time we arrive at the middle class home. First responders are there, the deputy is there, as are several neighbors. I get a quick version of the story from several of them before going into the house. The just of it being that the woman who lives in the house was abandoned by her husband after she had a psychotic episode several weeks ago. The neighbors are concerned because the woman, at least in their opinion, is unable to take care of herself.

"I tried talking to her," the deputy tells me, "She's definitely out of touch but she really hasn't done anything wrong. I called for you hoping you could talk her into going to the hospital."

"Well let's go in and see what's happening," I tell Robert.

We enter the open front door and immediately notice the carpet is sopping wet. No lights are on and I suspect the electricity has been turned off.

"Hello, anybody here?" I say in a loud voice.

"Yea, I'm back here in the kitchen," is the reply from a female voice. "Watch out for the snakes," she adds.

Robert and I exchange looks and make our way toward the voice. The house is a wreck, holes in the walls, doors off hinges, and broken windows in addition to the wet carpet.

Robert whispers to me, "I notice no one else bothered to come in with us."

"Yep, they're all a bunch a pansies."

We enter the kitchen to find a short chubby middle aged woman wearing a bathing suit standing by the back door with a water hose in her hand. She is spraying the kitchen cabinets but stops when she sees us.

"What's happening?" Robert asks in a friendly tone.

In just as friendly of a tone back she says, "Washing the snakes out of the house."

"It must have worked because I don't see any snakes," I tell her.

"They'll be back," she says.

"We're with the ambulance. Your neighbors are concerned about you and wanted us to check on you," Robert tells her.

Her mood immediately changes upon hearing this.

"Yea, I bet they're concerned. They won't even help me chase these damn snakes out of the house," she yells. "Where were they when my husband left two weeks ago? They didn't lift a finger when the unicorn got in and kicked holes in the walls. Concerned my ass," with that said she starts spraying the kitchen down again.

I notice she had cuts and bruises all over her legs and arms and think it might be a good way to get her to let us take her to the hospital. I hope this tactic will work since telling her she's crazier than a bed bug probably won't go over so well.

"Why don't you let us take you to the hospital? We'll have the doctors take a look at those cuts and bruises on your legs and arms."

Like most people who are out of touch with reality, she has an excuse for everything.

"If I go to the hospital who is going to keep the snakes and unicorns out of the house?"

I know arguing with her will not accomplish anything but try anyway, "We'll lock up the house and get the deputy to watch it."

"That deputy who came in here earlier?" she asks, "He'll leave as soon as we're gone and head for the donut shop."

She may be crazy, but that was funny, I think trying to keep a straight face.

Robert and I talk with her for a few more minutes without getting anywhere. It is obvious she will not go to the hospital willingly. We go back outside and tell the deputy what happened. The only thing that could be done would be for the deputy put her in protective custody.

"What about putting her in protective custody? Then I can go ahead and take her to the hospital," I ask the deputy.

"I really can't put her in protective custody. She's not really a threat to herself or others as far as I can see."

With that said he gets in his patrol car and leaves. Robert and I having no authority to make her go to the hospital reluctantly leave.

About a week later this poor woman set her kitchen on fire in a continued effort to rid the house of snakes. I didn't make the call but found out the deputy who came this time actually grew some guts and took her to the hospital to finally get her help she needed.

Local Entertainment

Rosie's Tea Room is quaint name for a small bar in an old predominately African American community in southern part of the county. You can't buy a cup tea there even if you want to but you can buy just about anything containing alcohol. For an extra charge you can also hire a woman that engages in the world's oldest profession.

As we turn in to the parking lot a bone thin young woman wearing a tube top and tight shorts is standing at the door of a house flagging us down.

"Well Robert, I never noticed this little house before," I tell him as we park the ambulance in front of a small shotgun house right next to Rosie's.

It's about 10:00 p.m. on a week night so there are only a few cars the parking lot. Being a small community a lot of people walk to Rosie's which at least cuts down on the drunk driving.

"What's the problem?" I ask the young woman at the door.

"She's floodin'," replies the skinny girl, as she opens the door and points to an old iron frame bed in the corner of the living room.

Flooding is an old term for vaginal bleeding.

It is a small room and I only have to take a few steps to get to the side of bed. I find another young woman lying there. In spite of it being a fairly warm night in a house with no air-conditioning she is covered up with a blanket.

"So young lady what's the problem tonight?"

"I be floodin'," the same answer I got from the other girl.

"How long have you been bleeding?" I ask.

"It dun started a couple of hours ago and ain't quit yet.

I notice she is very pale and appears to be weak. Even though she talks like one of the locals, it is obvious she is white. Of course lighter skinned African Americans can also be pale but they have to be in severe shock before you can see it. I am not certain, but assume she is one of the women that hang around the bar.

"Could you be pregnant?" A question I ask all women of child bearing age with this type of problem.

"Yes sir I could be."

I finish taking vitals, as I am taking the stethoscope out of my ears, I can hear Robert behind me talking to someone. My back has been to the door, so I turn around and am surprised at what I see. Robert is standing in the front door and just outside is a group of about 20 customers from Rosie's. Several are holding beers but all are craning their necks in an effort to see what is happening inside.

"Is the bitch goin to be alright?" I hear from somewhere in the crowd.

I now know for sure she is one of the "girls" from Rosie's. Being sarcastic I think. *It's overwhelming to see the love and compassion her customers have for her.*

Robert assures them that everything is under control and they slowly disperse.

All of her vitals and symptoms point to someone in hemorrhagic shock and we quickly start and IV and transport.

I found a few days later she had had a miscarriage. Even though she lost a lot of blood she recovered. I am sure her "customers" welcomed her back with open arms.

Modesty is in the Eye of the Beholder

Richard and I are shown to the bedroom of a tidy apartment. An elderly white haired woman propped up with several pillows is sitting in the bed.

Richard, who has just become a paramedic, is in charge of patient care. Since I am evaluating him before he is released to be an "in charge paramedic" he gets to ask the questions and decide on treatment while I watch and keep him from making any mistakes.

"What seems to be the problem?" Asks Richard.

"My chest feels funny," is her answer.

The questions and answers go back and forth for several minutes as Richard tries to get a history and an idea as to what is going on. Since her problem seems to be cardiac related, Richard decides to put grandma on the cardiac monitor.

As with all good paramedics, he tells his patient what he is about to do. Since the patient is an elderly woman Richard is especially concerned about protecting her modesty.

"I'm going to have to put these electrodes on your chest," he explains, "I have to put them in the right place so I need to get you to unbutton your pajama shirt just a little."

The patient unbuttons several buttons without hesitation practically exposing herself. Richard takes the first electrode and being careful not to move her shirt more than necessary sticks it on her right upper shoulder.

As he starts to place the second electrode the patient opens her shirt, fully exposing herself, and says, "Here honey, I don't mind if you see my boobs, I'm an old hussy from way back."

Richard doesn't know how to respond to this comment and frankly I didn't either. It's that you just don't think of prostitutes getting old.

.

Hamburgers and Harley's

Rancher Roy loads six Angus cows into his cattle trailer. He's in a hurry to get them to the auction barn and doesn't lock the trailer gate properly. Everything is going great until he swings his red Ford duly diesel truck onto the main highway without bothering to stop at the sign. Inertia forces the cows against the gate and it is forced open by their weight. The six large cows are thrown onto the busy highway. Three of cows are either dead or dying as they lie in the middle of the highway.

It's dusk and a middle aged couple with his and her Harley Davidson's are off on a weekend jaunt. The woman sees cars stopping and swerving in front of her and lets off on the motorcycle's throttle just before seeing a large black object lying directly in her path. She hits the brakes hard and does manage to slow down some before she collides with the cow.

316

The motorcycle stops abruptly upon hitting the half ton cow while the rider keeps on going. It's that inertia thing again. She goes over the handle bars does a half flip and by luck ends up landing on her back in the grassy median. Her companion was able to just skirt around the dead animal and come to a stop without wrecking.

In the meantime, a family of four in an old Dodge van hits a second cow and ramps over it becoming airborne just like the *General Lee* in what can best be described as a scene from *The Dukes of Hazard*.

We arrive to find dead cows, a twisted Harley, and a van with no front end. Except for the dead cows, everyone is up and walking around. We quickly hear the story of what happened. The part about the rancher not locking the trailer gate was told to me later that night by a deputy who investigated the accident.

We ended up transporting the woman who had been thrown from her motorcycle to the hospital as a precaution. She was more concern about her two grown children finding out she had bought a motorcycle than the minor injuries she had sustained.

Act of Compassion

It's a dark and foggy Friday night. A young co-ed from Texas A&M University is driving home for the weekend. As she rounds a long curve, a person comes into view. In the next micro second the young woman hits this person sending her into the windshield shattering it. The driver stops and runs back to find an elderly woman lying beside the road. The impact eviscerated the old woman and killed her immediately. The occupants of a nearby home hear the commotion and go outside to see what happened.

A middle-aged woman who lives in the house quickly realizes the person lying dead in the street is her mother.

Jason and I arrive to find the elderly victim already covered up with a sheet by her family. Since I never take a bystanders word that someone is dead we lift the sheet to check for ourselves. In this case it doesn't take a paramedic to realize she is gone.

The young co-ed is sitting in her car. We are told she has suffered cuts caused by the shattered windshield. As I talk to her, I quickly hear the story of what happened. Jason finds several deep cuts on her feet. It takes us a second to figure out what caused this. When the windshield shattered, shards of glass fell down into her shoes. When she ran back to see what she hit these shards were driven into her feet.

As expected the young woman is extremely upset knowing she has hit and killed someone. We have her in the back of the ambulance trying to pull the glass out of her wounds.

"Can I talk to her please?" a female voice asks through the back door.

"Yea, sure," I say not knowing she is the dead woman's daughter.

She gets in and sits down on the squad bench beside the patient.

"Listen to me," she says taking the young woman's hand, "It's not your fault. My mother had Alzheimer's and didn't know what she was doing or where she was. She got out of the house and we didn't know it. It's my fault for not keeping track of her, not yours."

With that said she gives the young woman a hug and leaves the ambulance.

This is still the biggest act of compassion I ever witnessed.

Horse Apples

"Man, its cold out here," I tell Karen as we head out the door of the station and into the ambulance.

"Quit your complaining. This feels good compared to summer when it's still eighty degrees at midnight," is Karen's quick response.

"You would think twenty eight degrees feels good. You're from Minnesota. It never gets above seventy there."

"I'm from Michigan, and you're wrong. Sometimes for a day or two in mid-summer it gets up to seventy two."

"Whatever, Michigan, Minnesota, it's one of those Yankee states that start with an M."

I know Karen is from Michigan but its fun to tease her about it.

Details are sketchy but we do know we are going to an auto accident involving a horse, never good combination. Horses being fairly tall animals tend to come back into the windshield of the vehicles that hit them. I have only made a few auto versus horse calls. In one the driver was crushed and killed and in the other the patient was scalped but lived. I have learned to expect the worst when responding to this type of call.

"You know I have come to look at car versus horse calls like auto versus trains," I tell Karen.

"How's that?" asks Karen.

"It seems like most of the patients of either scenario walk away from the accident or they are killed. There is no in between, its either life or death."

"Can't argue with that," replies Karen.

After about a twenty minute drive to the middle of nowhere, we finally see the lights of the patrol car. As usual the deputy is unable to give us any details in reference to injuries but was able to tell us to hurry up.

Karen has to maneuver around the dead horse to get us next to the old Chevy pickup that is sitting sideways in the roadway. As we pass, I can see that it has been eviscerated. There is steaming horse guts and manure all over the road. Karen and I both grimace.

"If the horse looks like that, I wonder what condition the patient is in," remarks Karen.

I was wondered the same thing.

As we approach the truck, I can also see steam rising from inside the truck. Just as I expected the truck's windshield is missing and the roof is bent in. I can see a middle aged man sitting in the driver's seat. He appears to be conscious and moving.

"It's about time y'all got here," complains the deputy, "Ben freezin' my ass off waiting for ya."

"We got hungry and had to stop at IHOP for breakfast. Would've brought you something but they ran out of donuts," I tell him as he turns and walks away without further comment.

Karen and I both have to pull on the truck door to get it open. While we do this the smell of steaming horse manure is almost over powering.

"Man this stinks," I say to no one in particular.

"If you think it's bad out there you should have been sitting in here for the past thirty minutes," the patient tells us.

We finally get the door open to find him covered from mid chest down in manure. In fact the seat and floor of the truck is also covered in steaming manure.

"I see what you mean," I tell him, "Do you hurt anywhere?" I ask.

I then notice fairly deep laceration on his forehead. It has quit bleeding but will definitely need a bunch of stitches.

"Just my head."

Since we can't see his legs and we have to get the patient out to transport. Karen and I start scooping the manure from around the patient with our latex gloved hands.

"You know it smells even more when you start stirring it up doesn't it?" I comment to the patient and Karen.

"Yea, just how much crap can one animal have inside him?" asks Karen rhetorically.

We finally get enough of it moved to get the patient out of the truck. He's lucky, his worst injury is the laceration. If he had been in a car or newer model truck he would have been scalped or possibility decapitated. At least he didn't get cold while he waited for the ambulance.

Epilog….One of the First

I am one of a handful of people who became some of first civilian paramedics in Texas way back in 1980. We fought for years to gain the confidence and trust of the nurses and doctors at the emergency rooms where we transported patients.

In the beginning we would show up with an IV already established and have the nurse ask us.

"Why did you start an IV?"

Now if a paramedic crew shows up without an IV they make the comment.

"Why didn't you start an IV?"

By the time I retired from EMS in the year 2000, paramedics were doing procedures we had only dreamed about twenty years before. Chest decompression, crycothyrodomies, cardiac pacing, and rapid sequence intubation to name a few. It took a while but paramedics are now an integral and respected part of the medical community.

I estimate that I responded to somewhere in the neighborhood of 7000 calls in my career. I figure that about half of these patients would have been just fine without the intervention of medical personnel. Although they were sick or injured or thought they were, they really didn't need an ambulance. When I first started riding on a volunteer ambulance in the mid 70s, we would bandage wounds, take vitals, settle arguments, provide psychological counseling, plus many other services. Then we would tell them to get in a car and go to the hospital or have someone take them. This let us return to service quickly and be available for real emergencies.

If there was any question at all we transported the patient in the ambulance. I always erred on the side of caution and transported the majority of my patients. Unfortunately a handful of medics abused this practice and refused to transport patients that really needed immediate medical attention. Within a few years most EMS services did not allow the paramedics to refuse to transport a patient. The patient had and still does have the right to refuse transportation.

It was my experience that if you responded to a sick call at two in the morning and the patient ends up not really wanting to go and you get a refusal you will probably be back out with in a hour or two on the same call. My philosophy was, "I'm up, someone's going to the hospital."

The next twenty five to thirty percent of the calls were people who needed transportation and medical care. The remaining twenty to twenty five percent were true emergencies.

In writing this book I tried to capture the full range of the type of calls I responded to. Yes, the majority of the stories are the exciting ones but I tried to include a few ordinary ones as well.

It may be hard to believe, but a majority of the calls followed a set routine. A paramedic has to be careful and not just assume a call is going to be routine. One of the worst mistakes you can make is to walk into a house and find the patient sitting with their bags packed and jump to the conclusion it's just someone wanting a taxi ride to the hospital. Just because they are prepared doesn't mean they aren't really sick. Yes, most of the time it is just someone wanting a taxi ride, but sometimes it's not. A good paramedic still takes the time to evaluate the patient.

With sick calls, which can be anything from bellyaches to headaches, paramedics usually just treat symptoms. Unless they are vomiting you can't give them anything for the belly pain and you certainly can't give them anything to get rid of the headache unless it is induced by high blood pressure. In this case you are treating the high blood pressure not the headache. You give them oxygen, get a medical history, start and IV, and transport.

It is also true that with most of the auto accidents I responded to no one was really hurt. Yes, they may be complaining of neck pain or back pain but the majority of the people did not have anything broken. I c-collared and back boarded them all unless they just flat refused transportation.

One patient I remember was one block from the hospital and had had slight fender bender. She was middle aged, and appeared to be wealthy. The car that rear ended her had no damage and we had a hard time finding a small scratch on the rear bumper of her car. Even though she had no actual complaints she would not make the decision to refuse transport. She insisted on me making the decision. In an effort to persuade her refuse treatment I explained that I would have to immobilize her even for a one block trip.

In the end we actually c-collared, back boarded, and transported for one block a person with no complaints of any kind. It would have been different if she had even complained of neck or back pain.

It was that small percentage of calls that were not routine where we earned our keep. I once heard an airline pilot's job described as "hours of boredom followed by a few moments of sheer terror." This pretty much sums up an emergency paramedics job.

People often ask me if being "burnt out" is the reason I retired as a paramedic. The answer to this question is "No."

On the day I retired, I still enjoyed helping people who were truly sick and injured. It was something I was good at and I always and still do enjoy helping people.

My last day as a paramedic was an exciting one. We had two saves.

The next morning I walked out of the station without ceremony. Twenty years sure go by quickly when you are having fun.

The End.

About the Author

I retired from EMS in 2000 since that time I have worked in the information technology field. I live in the suburbs north of Houston since 1970. I have been married for over 27 years to my one and only true love Tracey. We have one child Shawn who is now married and lives in the Dallas area.

Printed in Great Britain
by Amazon